For Michael.

A list of travelling
in the mind.

Liam

29/08/2024.

Remembering the Hippie Trail

travelling across Asia 1976–1978

Michael Hall

Published December 2007 by
Island Publications
132 Serpentine Road, Newtownabbey, Co Antrim BT36 7JQ, Northern Ireland

© Michael Hall 2007
mikehall.island@yahoo.co.uk

ISBN 978-1-899510-77-1

The author also publishes *Island Pamphlets*, a series of booklets which seek
to open up debate on historical, cultural, socio-economic, political and other
matters pertinent to Northern Ireland. Details can be found at
http://cain.ulst.ac.uk/islandpublications/

The author is grateful to Peter Pinney's daughter, Sava, for permission to quote
from his book *The Lawless and The Lotus* (1963). Readers might like to know
that Sava has made this title available again through www.lulu.com

Printed by Regency Press, Belfast

Contents

Cover photographs

Front cover

Top left: Some of the landscape near Göreme, in the Cappadocia region of central Turkey

Top right: Sheila surveying one of the lakes at Band-i-Amir, Afghanistan

Middle left: Sheila with the crew of a decorated lorry, Afghanistan

Middle right: Our view of Machhapuchhare and the Annapurna Himal from Pokhara, Nepal

Bottom left: Children from the Akha tribe, in the Golden Triangle area of northern Thailand

Bottom right: Our bus stuck in a mud-hole, while crossing the island of Sumatra, Indonesia

Back cover

Top left: Sheila hitchhiking through the North Island of New Zealand

Top right: Author at viewpoint overlooking Queenstown and Lake Wakatipu, in the South Island of New Zealand

Middle left: Striking rock formation in Hienghène Bay, New Caledonia

Middle right: The A-bomb dome, Hiroshima, Japan

Bottom left: Children dressed for a chilly Japanese winter, Japan

Bottom right: Women purchasing food supplies from one of the trains on the Trans-Siberian Railway, USSR

Europe

(21 July – 4 August 1976)

Even as the first rays of the morning sun woke me from my sleep, the uncomfortable nature of my position registered itself again at various parts of my body. The tangle of roots which had managed to irritate me throughout the night now sought to remind me of their presence. I was surprised that I had managed to fall asleep at all. As gently as I could I reached over to Sheila's sleeping-bag and slowly pulled aside the hood to uncover her head. I groaned inwardly when I saw her face: it was badly swollen, with hardly any part of it left unblemished by mosquito bites. Last night's efforts to clutch our sleeping-bags tightly around us had failed miserably – we had half-suffocated ourselves in our sweat-filled cocoons to no avail. Even though the uneven ground and overhanging branches had made it impossible to erect the tent, perhaps we should have just crawled inside its folds. Well, it was too late to be worrying about that now.

Sheila stirred and sighed. Had my movements woken her or had she been lying there half-awake? With another shock I realised that her left arm, which must have escaped the protection of her sleeping-bag during the night, was also badly swollen.

She turned towards me, pain clearly etched on her face. We gazed at each other for some moments, uncertain what to say. Perhaps it was fortunate that no words were indeed exchanged, for Sheila later admitted that she entertained serious doubts as to her desire to proceed with our long-haul venture. In retrospect, however, this was to be the only moment of hesitation we would experience over the next year and a half of travelling. But lying there, cramped and pained after a tormented night's sleep punctuated by the incessant buzzing of our relentless attackers, we might have been forgiven for this moment of uncertainty.

We slowly roused our aching bodies into sitting positions and leaned against our backpacks, feeling them damp with early morning dew. In the distance a lorry revved its engine but the surrounding undergrowth obscured our view of the outskirts of Niş, a grey industrial town in south-eastern Yugoslavia. The sound of the vehicle, however, was a reminder that our best plan of action now would be to find ourselves a suitable place to resume hitchhiking as soon as possible.

Bleary-eyed and dishevelled-looking we left the concealment of our forest bivouac and walked a short distance through a mass of tangled vegetation to the main road, along which we trudged for a hundred yards or so until we found a spot where cars would have a clear view of us and be able to pull in safely. If they should be so inclined, that is, for something told me that an opportunity to get away from here would not be presenting itself to us with any great urgency.

What traffic there was seemed predominantly local – tractors and lorries well laden with agricultural produce. Occasionally a battered old car would make an appearance, but we only thumbed these vehicles half-heartedly, assuming they were not going far. As they passed, their occupants would stare out in astonishment; even the first pedestrians heading into Niş would pause to stare at us from across the road, and our smiles were not always returned.

An hour passed and the sun rose rapidly in the sky. I looked around for tree cover which would serve as shade, but what was available was at a bad part of the road for hitching and we could not afford to put any obstacle in the way of a possible lift.

Another frustrating hour tediously passed. After having travelled so fast over the past few days we felt like sailors who, still heady after experiencing an exhilarating wind, now found themselves becalmed. We had disembarked from the Belfast to Liverpool boat at 7am on Wednesday and now, Monday morning, were almost through Yugoslavia, tantalisingly close to Greece. Not bad going, but then I had hitchhiked through Europe so often I almost knew the roads by heart: knew where the good and bad pitches were located; which routes and which cities to avoid; where the best hostels were and which hostels were not worth trudging to because their location necessitated a lengthy walk to the following day's pitch. Nor had we been delayed any more than usual at that notorious hitchhikers' bottleneck, the Frankfurter Kreuz, where two autobahns meet in a diabolical profusion and confusion of roads and slip-roads. I accept that the immense cloverleaf patterns these road junctions make must look stunningly beautiful from the air, but when viewed from behind a hitchhiker's hopefully raised thumb they are the stuff of nightmares.

But right now we were well and truly stalled, and one of the slow periods I had warned Sheila to expect – she being relatively new to this game – was upon us. For a while I wondered if I had read the road signs correctly when we trudged through the dark streets of Niş the previous night, for as yet we had seen little of the long-distance traffic normally to be expected on such a major trunk road. But gradually it built up, although it looked even less likely of providing us with onward transport than the local traffic, for most vehicles were filled to bursting with passengers and luggage. As I pondered our situation I broke one of hitchhiking's cardinal rules: I allowed myself to imagine that we could find ourselves still stranded here this evening. To a practised hitchhiker such a thought was sacrilege, for one should never begin to doubt one's luck until late in the afternoon, not even until dusk was finally approaching. Certainly not in the middle of the morning.

We had travelled so rapidly through Europe that in some countries we had not even needed to change currency to buy food, relying on supplies bought elsewhere. But now we had neither food to tide us over nor any Yugoslav currency with which to buy more. No hitchhiker, however, likes to vacate his pitch to go shopping, in case he misses a lift, even *the* lift, the one he has dreamed about for so long; although, as I surveyed the passing traffic, in our case it was more a concern about missing the *only* lift. Nevertheless, there was no point standing for hours without food.

"I think I'll head back into town and look for a bank. Sit over there in the shade, there's no point thumbing. Though if anyone *does* stop, and you see me returning along the road, maybe you could try and stall them a bit."

"Don't worry, I'll know what to do – I'm learning fast."

Behind Sheila's swollen face she managed a smile, and the fact that her spirits were obviously reviving despite her agony helped dispel my anxious mood. Why get uptight – we were only at the beginning of our journey, this was merely a slight hiccup and we had so much more ground to cover.

• • •

As I stood in line for one of the cashiers, I noticed another young foreigner nearby, counting his money, and I wondered if I could find an excuse to initiate conversation. My code of 'road ethics' prevented me from cadging lifts – at least by standing at the roadside you left the choice entirely to the driver – but nevertheless we *were* stuck. As he passed me I nodded a greeting, and assumed that he would understand English.

"Hi. Bloody hot, isn't it?"

My assumption was correct, for he responded in a strong Liverpudlian accent.

"Not half, mate; we're sweltering on our bus."

"You on public transport, then?"

"No, on a 'Magic Bus' to Athens."

My pulse quickened at this information but I tried to appear nonchalant.

"Packed, is it?"

He scrutinized me closely.

"You wanting a lift? Where are you going?"

"Wife and I are heading overland to Australia. But Athens would do for starters."

"I'm sure we could fit you in. You'd need to check it out with one of the drivers, though. We're parked a couple of hundred yards down the road."

To the surprise of the customer waiting in line behind me I immediately vacated the queue and exited the bank. I could see the bus in the distance and hurriedly made my way towards it. One of the drivers was scraping dead insects off the front windscreen and I quickly explained our predicament.

"No problem. Five US dollars each, is that okay? Look, we're just about to leave, so you hop on now and we'll pick up your missus as we drive out of town. Be a surprise for her."

He smiled mischievously and then seemed to ponder something more serious.

"There is just *one* problem though . . ."

He failed to finish the sentence and I waited expectantly, but he merely gestured dismissively with his hand.

"Never mind, you'll find out soon enough."

As the bus pulled in beside Sheila I could see her wave apologetically, indicating for it to proceed. But when I suddenly appeared at the doorway she jumped up in surprise and we hurriedly bundled our backpacks on board. In quite an ungainly manner we lugged our gear to the rear of the vehicle where we joined others already lying on a pile of mattresses, in a space created by the removal of the last few rows of seating. Once introductions had been made with our immediate neighbours we were soon appraised of the 'problem'.

Magic Buses had originated in the 1960s to cater for the growing number of young people – hippies, 'freaks' and shoestring travellers – who were 'on the road', seeking adventure, companionship and a sense of untrammelled freedom. Some were owned by former hippie-travellers who felt it an ideal way to subsidise their freewheeling lifestyle, and were the forerunners of the adventure-tour companies which would later emerge. These buses carried young Europeans to destinations all over their own continent, invariably places considered to be definitely 'in' with carefree youth – Amsterdam, Copenhagen, Athens. Some, however, went further afield – to Afghanistan, India and Nepal. We had toyed with the idea of travelling to India on such a bus, but the thought of being tied to the same vehicle seemed far too restricting, and we also wanted to take as much time over the journey as we needed.

The owner of this particular bus, before starting out on his present journey, had been approached by a more up-market travel company which had gone bust and was anxious to get its customers – a group of middle-class, middle-aged Greek businessmen and their wives – fixed up with transport home to Greece. The Magic Bus owner had warned the other company about the type of passengers he normally transported, but they either did not comprehend or did not care.

When the two sets of passengers encountered one another conflict was almost guaranteed. Not a national or a cultural conflict as such, more a generational one, a clash of lifestyles. A focus for the conflict was provided by the music constantly played over the PA system. Being a Magic Bus this music – mostly heavy rock followed by more heavy rock – did not simply drift pleasantly through the speakers, but reverberated deafeningly without respite. It had quickly become too much for the Greeks and they had rebelled. Heated arguments erupted until a compromise was reached: one Greek tape to follow every heavy rock tape. The problem with this, however, was that the Greeks possessed only *one* tape of Greek music, and after it had been played a half-dozen times it was the turn of the young people to rise in revolt. Matters had still not been resolved when we joined this divided band of travellers, and the tenseness in the atmosphere was almost palpable.

The 'problem' was eventually resolved in dramatic fashion. During the night, having crossed into Greece, we passed a small seaside town whose beach glittered invitingly in the moonlight, and with gleeful insistence the driver was made to stop – not that he needed much persuading – while his youthful passengers tumbled off the vehicle.

Then, to our amazement, those racing down to the beach began to divest themselves hurriedly of every stitch of clothing. The Greek passengers were aghast – things had been bad, but skinny-dipping in the Aegean was taking things just a bit too far! Sheila and I followed down to the water's edge, paddling in the gently breaking surf and feeling each retreat of the sea suck small pebbles from beneath our feet with a gentle, caressing motion.

When all the contented revellers returned to the bus it was to find that the Greeks, having discovered an all-night taxi depot nearby, had decided to undertake the remainder of their journey in less scandalous company.

A few hours before dawn we found ourselves bedding down on a rooftop mattress in Athens and drifting off into a long-desired sleep.

• • •

Our decision to embark upon an extensive overland journey had a certain inevitability about it. From my early teens my daydreams had been filled with images of foreign lands and ancient cultures. At weekends I scoured Belfast's second-hand bookshops for titles on world travel and the exploits of explorers and adventurers, longing for the time when I too could head off to far-flung destinations.

Furthermore, among young people in the 1960s another journey was often talked about – the inward journey – and like many of my contemporaries I delved into Zen, meditation, yoga, and, most potent of all, experimentation with the 'mind-expanding' drug LSD. Much of the so-called hippie scene was undoubtedly shallow and little different from other fads, but for many young people the quest for self-knowledge was perfectly genuine. And when you combined a desire to travel with the search for inner knowledge, it automatically pointed in one direction – a journey to the East.

Even for those not enamoured by talk of inner quests, in the late 1960s and early 1970s an obsession with settling down and securing a career and a mortgage was well down one's list of priorities. There was a mood of self-sufficiency about, not based on having money in the bank, but on confidence in one's own ability to survive and adapt. Among many young people the desire to 'get up and go' was stronger than the inclination to simply stay at home and vegetate. My readings may have fuelled my appetite for long-haul travelling in a manner absent from Sheila's experience, but her willingness to embark upon our venture was just as evident. This was epitomised by her reaction when I showed her the route I proposed we take to India and back. She scrutinized the world map for some moments, lost in thought. She had never expressed any hesitation up to now and her seriousness perturbed me.

"Are you happy enough with that?" I asked her, somewhat anxiously.

She leaned over the map and stretched her thumb and little finger to touch both Ireland and India, then moved her hand sideways so that her thumb and finger, still held the same distance apart, now touched India and Australia. She looked up, a clear determination etched upon her features.

"There hardly seems any point retracing all our steps from India when the same distance will take us to Australia?"

I smiled and watched as she continued to peruse the map, suspecting what was coming next.

"And, furthermore, there hardly seems any point retracing our steps from Australia when we can just continue on round."

Quite logical, really, when you think about it.

• • •

The Greek island of Samos was to be our last European port of call before setting foot in Asia, and it was on Samos that we allowed ourselves to unwind after our headlong dash through Europe. A dash necessitated mainly by Europe's high cost of living. We had lived in Amsterdam for over a year and saved sufficient money, so we hoped, to see us through Asia, and the idea of having to make a sizeable dent in those savings right at the beginning of our travels was unthinkable.

It was on Samos too that we decided to reassess the weight we were carrying. Years of hitchhiking experience in Europe had taught me to trim the contents of my backpack down to the essentials. But to set off half-way around the world was stepping into the unknown, and we had included items we thought we *might* need, but had no way of telling if we *would*. The heaviest item was a tent. On my previous travels, whenever I failed to make it to a hostel or was running low on finances, I would bed down close to the main road using whatever concealment – forest, hedge, outhouse – came to hand. For those situations I used a plastic bivi-bag, into which I would stuff my sleeping-bag and then crawl inside. Usually after an energetic day's hitchhiking sleep came rapidly and the lack of grandeur of one's sleeping arrangements was irrelevant. However, for our Asian trip a tent had seemed more appropriate, and yet we wondered whether we would have many opportunities to use it.

This reassessment had been occasioned when, on our first day on Samos, we set out to visit Zoodóhos Pigí monastery, situated atop Mount Rabaidoni, and carrying everything with us. Despite our thoughts being largely preoccupied with the magnificent panorama of sea and coastline below us, we rapidly began to tire. Eventually we felt so exhausted that we collapsed against a rough stone wall where the nearby olive trees cast at least a token semblance of shade across the roadway.

"This heat's unbelievable! I can't see us lugging our gear up to this monastery, never mind all the way across Asia!"

Sheila did not reply, but peered intently into the olive grove.

"What about hiding our rucksacks in there for the moment; I'm sure they'd be safe enough."

"Okay, and while we're at it, let's see what we can dump."

Locating a clear patch of ground we emptied the contents of our backpacks and attempted the near-impossible: paring down what had already been pared down.

"These plastic plates can go – right?"

I looked at Sheila for agreement; she just shrugged her shoulders.

"One spare pair of socks should be enough? And when we buy sandals . . ."

Despite our best rationalisations the bundle of to-be-ditched items remained pitifully small. Out went a bottle of Mandle's Throat Paint Solution given to me by a retired British Indian Army officer as a way of preventing throat infections in dusty or desert-like conditions. Out went items of clothing: "There's bound to be plenty of cheap clothes in India?"

Finally we concealed our not-too-much-lighter backpacks in the olive grove, and, leaving the to-be-abandoned items on a wall outside a house where we had espied some teenage girls, we resumed our trek to the monastery. I flexed my aching shoulders, now thankfully free of their oppressive burden, and looked at Sheila.

"It's still bloody hot, isn't it!"

• • •

The heat was indeed hard to adjust to and our five-day sojourn on Samos was spent either cooling off in the sea, hiding from the sun, tending to our sunburn, or searching for standpipes which actually had water flowing from them. Not the most carefree start to our adventure but nevertheless we felt ourselves slowly unwinding, and hopefully our bodies were gradually acclimatising to conditions far removed from the often chilly weather of home – although there were times when we longed for a drop of Irish rain.

The friendliness of the local people, however, compensated to a large degree for our physical discomfiture. Even the young soldiers we encountered – and there were many in evidence with this being the closest Greek island to Turkey – were talkative and friendly. On one occasion, when we went to a seemingly deserted cove and began to change into our swimwear, a polite cough suddenly startled us. We spun around but to our astonishment could see no-one, until an army officer slowly emerged from an extremely well-camouflaged dugout only yards away and waved a greeting before slowly disappearing once again. We wondered whether any young conscripts in the dugout with him were cursing this spoiled opportunity for a bit of voyeurism.

• • •

The port of Pithagório – on the southern coast of Samos – was one of those attractive but restful places which prove that travel brochures do not always lie. It was also one of those places you hoped would not actually appear on too many such brochures, for there were few tourists about to disturb its tranquillity or distract our attention from the absorbing scenes of local people going about their daily toil. One focus of our fascination was provided by a group of fishermen sorting out their nets along the quayside, the dense mesh of the nets blurring into a misty splash of golden brown, which contrasted vividly with the different blues which adorned the fishing boats gently bobbing up and down in the foreground.

As we sat outside a taverna contentedly sipping coffee and surveying this kaleidoscope of colours, Sheila dutifully penned letters home while I again perused our new student cards with some satisfaction. Travelling 'on a shoestring' encourages you to pursue all opportunities to cut down on costs. A student card accorded the holder excellent travel reductions in certain countries, including 20% on Turkey's trains and a generous 50% on Indian railways. Even though we were not students I saw no reason why we should not possess these money-saving documents.

Now, in the three years since I had gained a degree from Queen's University Belfast, I had been sent an annual invitation to a convocation of former graduates. Usually these invites ended up in the rubbish bin – but not the last one. Using the letter – emblazoned with the university's logo – as my base, I had pasted a new paragraph over the original invite, this paragraph explaining 'to whom it concerns' that Sheila and I were bona fide students on two years' sabbatical leave, studying Asian culture. Talcum powder was rubbed around the edges of the new paragraph and when the page was photocopied the join-lines miraculously disappeared.

During our stay in Athens we had visited a travel agent through whom replacement student cards could apparently be obtained, and explained that, although our original cards had been stolen, we had in our possession a letter which confirmed our student status. The girl at the counter had perused it solemnly and then nodded affirmatively.

"No problem; your replacement cards will be ready tomorrow."

"Thank you. It was fortunate that we hadn't lost that letter too."

The girl had looked at me with a barely-concealed smile.

"Yes, I suppose it is. Of course, we could have got you new cards without it, but we would have had to charge you more."

• • •

If the turbulence in the water could be described as a heavy swell within the sheltered area of the harbour at Samos-town, out at sea it was quite a different story, for there the waves tumbled about with a virulent and reckless abandon. It was such seas which had been detaining us on Samos for the past few days. After our leisurely circuit of the island we had returned to Samos-town only to learn that the boat to Kuşadasi in Turkey, the cheapest one available, had broken down. The following day, finding that this boat was still out of commission, we reluctantly agreed to take a more expensive one, but ten minutes before *its* planned departure the police had intervened and refused permission for it to leave because of the extremely high seas. A heated quayside argument between the boat owners and the police had ensued, with the police finally relenting, though insisting that anyone taking to sea in such a small craft in such weather must sign a disclaimer accepting full responsibility for their actions. That was enough to cause most of the prospective passengers to lose confidence and agree to wait a further day.

And now today, with the seas appearing to be somewhat calmer, and the passengers finally boarding the boat after a two-hour bureaucratic hassle with the police which had seemed routine rather than out of the ordinary, it was discovered that *our* two passports, which had been deposited with the police the day before, were the only ones not to materialise again. More frantic toing and froing ensued until they were finally unearthed.

Then the boat had hardly left the safety of the quayside when the self-winding gear broke down and the anchor had to be winched up solely by hand and Greek curses, the vessel taking the opportunity to pirouette around the harbour to the great amusement of shore-bound onlookers.

Once out in the open sea the relative calm of the harbour was replaced by a violent lurching as the first waves pummelled over the bow. The skipper's hoarse order for all passengers to go below was unnecessary, for those of us in the bow area were already scurrying aft, our backpacks tangling with obstacles as we bundled them along the narrow deck space, our hands grasping for any fixtures we could hold on to. A forceful curse erupted from a Spaniard behind me as our halting progress caused him to be drenched by a massive wave. I half-turned to apologise but decided against it and pushed on past coils of rope and other obstructions until we finally made the relative protection of the small cabin area.

As the boat swayed drunkenly in the fierce swell and the glass in the portholes threatened to split asunder with each crashing wave, a few of our fellow-passengers edged closer to the door of the boat's only toilet, and there was a noticeable paling of the golden Greek tan some had acquired. A young American beside us ran his hands through his hair and peered anxiously out at the raging seas.

"Jesus, I'm sure glad we didn't go yesterday, after all."

I followed his gaze through the porthole, our lurching movements making the retreating island visible, now invisible, now visible again . . . The American nervously fidgeted with the straps on his backpack, which he gripped tightly between his knees.

"I sure hope we won't be driven back – something definitely seems to be trying to prevent us leaving Samos."

Turkey

(4–20 August 1976)

Early afternoon in Kuşadasi was hot, almost unbearably hot, and as those parts of the town we walked through looked too touristy we easily convinced ourselves not to linger but to take a minibus – a *dolmus* – to the village of Selçuk, from where we could visit the ancient city of Ephesus.

The Graeco-Roman ruins at Efes are impressive and extensive. At first we dutifully located each section of the ruins on a small guide-map, reading interesting facts aloud to one another. But eventually we desisted from this and simply meandered among the fallen stones and gleaming columns. This was to be the pattern right across Asia. Although we endeavoured to gather whatever information we could about a temple or a monument before actually visiting it, once we arrived there we were content to soak up the atmosphere, observe the faithful at their devotions, savour the myriad smells, feast our eyes upon the splurge of colour, watch the light play patterns over delicate carvings, listen to the cacophony of sounds . . . or just relax in the stillness and the silence.

I often wonder, when reading those travel books which every so often transmogrify into history books crammed with endless facts and dates, whether the authors really knew all these details while actually visiting the places concerned, or whether they were filled in later to add a sense of scholarship to their writing. Certainly we knew enough about each location to establish its historical and cultural significance, but we felt no desire to be overburdened with facts, dates and personalities. Anyway, most facts and dates relate to the doings of kings and generals, and we were more interested in the lives of ordinary people. To watch, listen, smell, touch – that was all we ever felt was really needed.

Dusk found us wandering around the outskirts of Selçuk again, searching for a secluded spot to bed down for the night. A graveyard with a low concealing wall seemed to offer the most seclusion, but we hesitated.

"I wonder if local people would consider it a sacrilege if we were to sleep in there?"

A villager and his son approached and stopped to stare. I smiled and raised my hand in greeting.

"Hello. Is it permissible . . . ah, is okay? . . . to sleep in there?" After pointing to the graveyard, I rested my head against my pressed-together palms, but the man simply smiled and noisily spat out whatever it was he had been chewing.

"We wish to sleep in there. No problem?" I closed my eyes and tilted my head again in a poor resemblance of someone asleep.

This time he began nodding positively, though whether he had the faintest idea as to what these two backpack-laden foreigners wanted was hard to ascertain – perhaps he thought my miming referred to the permanent state of rest enjoyed by the present residents of the graveyard. He finally moved on at a leisurely pace, while his son followed by his side, walking backwards and not diverting his bright staring eyes from ours. Eventually they both fell out of sight beyond a turn in the road. The light was fading rapidly even as we stood there, our tiredness was increasing and we needed to make a decision. We took one last scrutinising look around and climbed over the wall.

• • •

We were abruptly startled from our sleep by a muezzin's early morning call to prayer, his amplified voice bellowing forth from a loudspeaker high up on the minaret of a nearby mosque. The sound was so penetrating we made a mental note to check for the proximity of mosques the next time we found ourselves with a choice of accommodation.

We had originally lain down to sleep in just our sleeping-bags but mosquitos threatened to complete what they had begun in Yugoslavia and eventually we had crawled inside the tent folds, holding the material away from our faces by means of a guy-line attached to the stone wall.

As we made ready to set forth we were in good spirits, noting a definite sense of anticipation for whatever lay ahead. Even during our stay on Samos we had not felt as if our journey had really commenced, but now, with the muezzin's call still echoing in our ears and the sight of a small boy shepherding a herd of goats up a hillside track above us, we could believe that our travels had at last begun.

. . .

Our first encounter with Turks had actually been in Yugoslavia. We had entered Yugoslavia in a brand new Mercedes, its driver a Jordanian who had purchased the vehicle in Germany and was intending to sell it at a profit in his home country. He paid scant regard to the normal practice of 'running in' a new vehicle, for where he could he belted down the road at between 80 and 90 miles per hour. And where he could not attain this speed, it was only because of an amazing situation. The roads were congested with thousands of Turkish 'guest workers' returning home from Germany on holiday. The scenes at the Austrian/Yugoslav border had been indescribably chaotic, while along the open road matters seemed frenzied. Where the road allowed vehicles to pass – and even where it did not – drivers weaved in and out like men possessed. Every lay-by was bunged with broken-down or overheated vehicles, their occupants encamped alongside like tribes of itinerants. Occasionally, mangled vehicles lay entwined around one another, while the Yugoslav helicopters circling overhead – no doubt trying to make some sense of it all – compounded the totally surreal quality of it all. It was an amazing movement of humanity, with all the appearance of an entire people fleeing some natural or man-made disaster.

. . .

Wanting to visit the natural wonder of Pamukkale, we boarded a train to Gonçali. The journey to Gonçali, so we had been told, would take between two and three hours to complete – in fact it took seven, and we realised we must have inadvertently taken either the *posta* (mail train) or the *yolcu* (local). Nevertheless, we were glad of our mistake, for it proved to be a fascinating and rewarding journey.

At every halt vendors of all ages ran alongside the carriages, vociferously advertising their wares. A family of migrant workers bundled themselves into our compartment, complete with chickens, bags of grain and assorted family ornaments amongst their luggage. They spoke no English but were spontaneously friendly, the children shy and very good-looking. Throughout the journey, as word of our presence spread along the train, many of the other passengers would come to the door of our compartment and attempt conversation. Those whose English was nonexistent would just stand and smile. We felt somewhat awed by their curiosity and friendliness and did our best to respond to each gesture, each smile, each fumbled question, endeavouring to ensure than none of these warm-hearted people had any cause to feel slighted.

The friendship of our fellow passengers more than compensated for the tedium of the journey and there were only two real problems. Firstly, the heat, which was as intense in late afternoon as it had been at noon – even when we stuck our heads out of the window all we were rewarded with was a blast of hot air. Secondly, the choking black smoke, which billowed forth from the steam locomotive and completely enveloped our compartment each time we went through a tunnel. When we eventually disembarked at Gonçali we felt absolutely filthy on the outside, but inwardly aglow from the intensity of our experience.

At Gonçali we changed trains for the shorter journey to Denizli. At Denizli we stood on the station platform studying the timetable, hoping to make plans for our onward travel a few days' hence. Unfortunately, it completely baffled us and our long scrutiny eventually attracted the attention of the stationmaster. When our attempt at communication proved futile, he indicated for us to wait, then he hurried off, to return a few minutes later with a youth in tow. This youth, the stationmaster's nephew, spoke perfect English and soon sorted out our queries.

When we informed him that we were bound for Pamukkale he requested to accompany us, for he was on holiday with little else to do. Unable to get a bus due to the lateness of the hour, our new companion hailed a taxi for which he insisted on paying.

Pamukkale is a remarkable place. Hot underground springs had brought a high concentration of dissolved mineral salts to the earth's surface, and as the water flowed downhill it cooled and evaporated, depositing the dissolved minerals. The result was tier upon tier of gleaming white terraces, their overlapping basins resembling a series of petrified waterfalls.

There was a campsite nearby and despite failing to find the person in charge – we never did find anyone – we proceeded to erect our tent. Those who travel around independently know the slight sense of anxiety which can arise when daylight is fading and no definite place for the night has been located. They can equally appreciate the peace of mind which is experienced when a room has been found, or a campsite reached, and all made ready for the night. It was in such a state of contentment that we sat for the next few hours engrossed in conversation with our new companion.

Ufuk Sarioğlu was as glad of our company as we were of his, for he had frequently found himself isolated within his own community. A member of a small Communist grouping, he had spent a week in jail for helping to organise a People's Concert. As a Communist he was viewed with distrust and even distaste by some local Muslims, as well as being labelled a traitor for disagreeing with Turkey's war with Greece over Cyprus. Not that he minded, for he seemed to relish confrontations: knowing that his pale complexion made him look like a foreigner he told us how he would trick vendors at food markets into believing he was a tourist, to see if they would grossly overcharge, then lambast them for their greed.

However, it was not in Turkey where he had received his greatest upset. In a desire to escape the rigidities of his own culture he had travelled around Europe, eventually falling in love with a Dutch girl. By the cruelest of ironies, the parents of this girl were, untypical for the liberal Netherlands, members of an extremely narrow-minded Protestant sect. They disliked their daughter's relationship with Ufuk intensely, not merely on religious grounds but with a strong dose of racism, and eventually managed to destroy it. Ufuk returned home much disheartened, although the experience had obviously not embittered him or left him any less generous in spirit.

•   •   •

As I lay awake, listening to the incessant chirping of the crickets – at least it was better than the irritating drone of mosquitos – I reflected upon Ufuk's circumstances and upon our own. Sheila was born a Catholic and I was baptised a Protestant – although I never came to see myself as one – and in the Northern Ireland of the early 1970s mixed relationships not only risked family upsets but courted sectarian antagonism. Although I was vehemently opposed to the idea that our intended marriage needed the blessing of *any* church, I relented because of the unnecessary stress this stance imposed upon Sheila.

Knowing that her own parish priest would not look kindly upon our union, and having lived away from home for many years, Sheila had been free to approach any priest she choose, and assumed that the one who ministered to the Catholic students attending Queen's University, Belfast's premier seat of learning, would be reasonably enlightened in his attitude.

I had waited in the car outside the parochial house and it was a much subdued Sheila who returned a short time later.

"Do you want to know the extent of his pastoral concern? Or of his ability to relate to my worries? Or of his interest in you as a prospective husband and father, even a possible convert? He wasn't even concerned whether we loved each other; he merely asked one question: 'Can you not find yourself a good Catholic?'"

Sheila approached another Catholic clergyman, only to be met with a similarly negative stance. As we had been talking about going to Amsterdam to look for work, we now decided to do so – and got married in England on our way there. Unknown to us then, we had taken the first step towards our present journey.

•   •   •

There was something about the look of the crowd waiting outside the mosque which instantly alerted me. Before I could turn round to warn Ufuk the three of us were quickly surrounded, and, with an intensity which alarmed me, a string of abuse suddenly emanated from the most vociferous members of the gathering, mainly directed at Ufuk.

This sudden hostility took Sheila and I completely by surprise, not least because we had just passed two of the most relaxing days imaginable: dining alfresco beside our tent on sumptuous feasts of bread, yoghurt, cheese, tomato and water melon; swimming in the public pool at Pamukkale filled with the warm mineral water; lazily exploring the nearby Roman ruins of Hieropolis; but most of all just whiling away the hours in animated conversation. Yet now, back in Denizli prior to resuming our onward journey, we were being confronted by an angry, gesticulating crowd.

Although I could not understand a word that was being exchanged, I suspected it had something to do with our visit to the mosque. Ufuk at one stage even appeared to be enjoying the situation – and was certainly giving as much, and just as loudly, as he was getting – until he seemed to remember our presence and glanced quickly towards us. Perhaps the sight of our anxious faces chastened him, for when he turned again to the crowd his tone was more conciliatory, his hand gestures less threatening. In the hope that it would be of assistance to him, I gave a disarming smile to anyone I found gazing directly at me. Finally the crowd, still grumbling its irritations, gradually began to move away and a deeply embarrassed Ufuk turned to face us.

"I am so sorry for bringing this trouble upon you."

"What on earth was it all about!"

"It did not concern you two. Some of those people had been in the mosque when I was showing you around and were offended that I made no attempt to pray. It is just this . . . this religious thing . . . oh, how can I explain?"

I laughed reassuringly at his obvious discomfiture.

"To us? And us from Northern Ireland? No need to explain."

As we walked away, however, there was no denying that the incident had been deeply unsettling. I had been personally confronted by bitter sectarian hostility on a number of occasions back home – including having had gunshots fired in my direction – but no amount of such incidents ever prepares you for the turbulence your entire nervous system experiences.

Almost as if he was aware of our still-quaking dispositions, a nearby barber – who had seemingly observed the whole incident – energetically beckoned us over.

"Come in, come in – you must sit and have some çay with me. Come!"

Without hesitation we joined him – indeed, it would probably have proven more difficult to elude the barber's insistent invite than to have evaded the angry crowd. The four of us chatted at great length, drinking endless cups of tea, and our recent scare became gradually submerged and forgotten through this reaffirmation of Turkish hospitality.

When we finally said our farewells to a regretful Ufuk and took the train to Afyon and then on to Eskişehir, that hospitality was almost to overwhelm us. In the station at Eskişehir we had to wait two and a half hours for a train to Ankara, and during that time we were constantly surrounded by groups of friendly Turks, proffering endless handshakes, insisting upon numerous exchanges of addresses, and engaging us in a non-stop string of conversations. At one stage we had been dragged, despite our protestations, to the front of the ticket queue – we were tourists, after all, seeing their country. As we were pushed past the others waiting in line I smiled apologetically and tried in vain to halt our progress, but no-one seemed to mind and the only response was yet more smiles.

Children were prodded and cajoled by proud parents into trying out their English, and for the sake of that pride we made a real effort to grasp what the children were saying, and even when comprehension eluded us we pretended to understand and 'conversed' with the delighted youngsters. Anyway, the glowing faces of those children was itself an international language which required no translation. People showed us photographs of their families and asked us if we carried photographs of ours. Others asked us about our country and whether we liked theirs. There was no respite during those long two hours, no saturation point on their part and new faces kept being added to the gathering all the time. Even when the train finally departed, it was not over yet, for children and young people ran alongside our carriage, waving and calling out their goodbyes.

We sat in the carriage totally dazed, completely lost for words. Something about it had almost seemed unreal, and yet in no way could that be a fair description, for it was its very realness which left us now feeling quite emotional. Many hippies and travellers sped through Turkey en route to Iran and beyond, but we had wanted to see more of the country and its people. We had not anticipated such a reception, however, and realised that it would have been a terrible mistake to have missed out on all of this.

Even in the capital, Ankara, we were instantly approached by helpful Turks whenever we stopped to peruse our street map. Our only fear was that some day the growing impact of tourism – and the rude attitudes displayed by many travellers – would eventually begin to undermine all this warm-heartedness. But for now, we revelled in it and tried to make our hosts feel that it was more than appreciated.

· · ·

The extraordinary landscape of Cappadocia is truly unique. All over this vast fairytale landscape – which lies near the centre of Turkey on the Anatolian plateau – cones and pyramids of soft rock stand in a profusion which in places seems quite surreal. Among the tall pinnacles of rock – some as high as 160ft – a few are incongruously capped with black conical boulders of weather-resistant basalt. In one particular location a few of the pinnacles are surmounted by two or three stems with conical caps, popularly referred to as 'fairy chimneys'. Even more startling amid this weird, moon-like landscape, is that many of these rock-cones show evidence of human habitation, with openings for windows and doors cut into them at different levels.

The legacy of a sustained Christian settlement is also much in evidence, with the discovery of some 400 churches hewn out of the rock, from simple chapels to large sanctuaries decorated with elaborate frescos.

Our base in the region was the small, friendly town of Ürgüp. We had travelled there by bus from Ankara, which proved to be much cheaper than the train. Our final stage to Ürgüp was by *dolmus* and as we were getting out of the vehicle we were approached by a solitary hotel owner. This in itself was quite unusual, for normally upon arrival at train and bus stations in Asia travellers are bombarded by a deafening deluge of taxi-men, hotel reps and private bus company touts, all competing in unison for their attention. The room he offered was too pricey, but he agreed to let us camp in his garden for much less. Still buoyant from our recent encounter with Turkish hospitality we succumbed to his insistence that we take at least one in-house meal – as we were his "guests" – and that meal cost us four times the camping fee! Even hospitable people can learn how to fleece tourists, we moaned.

However, any irritation we felt soon dissipated when, wandering around Ürgüp that evening, a metalsmith, hailing us as we passed his workshop, invited us in for *çay* and then delighted us by playing hauntingly beautiful music on his *saz* – a long-necked lute.

· · ·

"Where are they taking us?"

I could detect a noticeable anxiety in the German girl's voice and I must admit I was not immune to a growing unease myself, but one of our hosts smiled reassuringly and I allowed any doubts to subside.

Our musician host of yesterday had informed us that some of his friends, all males in their early twenties, had invited five young travellers – four females and one male – to a midnight music and *sis kebab* party. Agreeing to join them we had squeezed ourselves, amid much merriment, into three cars and set off into the darkness along a bumpy country road. After travelling for some considerable distance we parked beside a dark rockface and alighted from our vehicles, glad to be able to stretch our cramped legs. As our hosts led us through the darkness we realised that this rockface, like so many others in the area, was honeycombed with deserted dwellings. In silence and with an anticipation tempered with uncertainty – it was then that one of the two German girls had voiced her concern – we ascended a rough stone stairway, and, bending low, eventually emerged into what must have passed for the former main room of a troglodyte house.

Earlier that day, as Sheila and I had set out on a leisurely exploration of the astonishing landscape around Göreme – eating liberally of the apricots which grew in abundance all around – we had wondered what these dwellings would have been like to live in. Now, with the interior of our party venue soon lit by the warm flickering glow of strategically placed candles, I realised that with the addition of a few basic comforts – such as carpets and cushions – they could be made very pleasantly habitable.

Our jovial hosts soon had a fire going and in minutes skewered meat began to sizzle, its aroma stimulating our growing hunger pangs. Then the music commenced: rhythmic, almost hypnotic music, of a type which made me want to close my eyes and relax, not find myself forced into gregarious activity. Such as the dancing, which no-one was allowed to sit out.

The former apprehensions relaxed as the party got under way, and drink and an abundant supply of nuts supplemented the music and *sis kebab*. Sheila and I politely declined the drink, a wise decision in retrospect, for it soon became obvious that our hosts' real aspirations – should we not have suspected this all along? – was to get off with all the females. One even asked Sheila if she would like him to accompany her "outside to the toilet".

Not only were my hands soon fully occupied fending off male attentions directed towards Sheila, but I repeatedly had to intervene on behalf of the other females, doing so firmly but with as little sign of aggression as I could. For some reason I imagined that the risks inherent in our predicament could be minimised if we all managed to stay together, and my fear was that some of the females would be cajoled – or dragged – out of my sight into another room. This would leave me and the other male with a near-impossible situation to oversee. But fortunately this did not occur and instead our group gravitated into a tight defensive bunch – still putting on a show of dancing, with everyone trying, with decreasing success, not to take too much notice of the amorous attentions of our hosts. Around the outside of the group the young males hovered expectantly – and showed signs of becoming increasingly irritated.

This stand-off continued for another hour until repeated demands from the upset females to be taken home finally convinced the youths that tonight they were out of luck. In angry retaliation they demanded money from each person to cover the food and drink, working out a price per head. Sheila and I would have gladly paid up just to get away – and, anyway, it had been far better value than our previous night's hotel meal – but our musician friend, who had obviously not been party to his friends' real intentions and had looked decidedly embarrassed throughout, persuaded his companions to accept a lesser amount for both of us.

When we were finally deposited back in Ürgüp the two German girls, whose original ambition had been to sleep out under the stars in one of the empty dwellings – imagining it would be, as one of them had said, "so romantic" – were by now thoroughly frightened and bedded down in our hotel garden beside our tent.

• • •

This incident was not the first, nor the last, time we would encounter sexual harassment. The Turkish male's approach to Western females could be quite unsettling. The incident at Ürgüp was admittedly unpleasant, but, for us at least, it was somewhat untypical. A more usual encounter would be far less dramatic and much less threatening. And each incident invariably took us

29

by surprise, either because of our naivety or because we were so accustomed to most encounters with Turks being friendly and hassle-free.

Once, while on a train and with our map of Turkey spread out between us and an inquisitive Turk, Sheila suddenly stiffened, a startled look across her face. I immediately lifted the map – which had been lying across all our knees – to find our companion's hand gently caressing her thigh. He looked at me and I responded by shaking my head reproachfully. He immediately removed his hand, nodded understandingly, and then continued his exploration of our itinerary as if nothing untoward had happened. On another occasion a *dolmus* driver offered us a free lift when he saw us being transported on the trailer of a tractor. We were glad to accept, for the unsolicited trailer ride was juddering our rib-cages so painfully we feared another few miles could have left us with internal bruising. The *dolmus* driver, on reaching his destination, insisted upon buying us a meal and then sat chatting over cups of *çay*. At one stage I left to visit the toilet and when I returned I could see from Sheila's livid expression that she had been receiving yet more unwelcome attention. I angrily rounded on our companion, and he smiled apologetically – and then, just as we had come to expect, resumed his friendly conversation.

It was all very disconcerting. It was as if Turkish men felt obliged to try their hand with all foreign females – on the assumption that the sexually liberated image attached to Western women meant that anyone was free to touch them up. Yet, once rebuked, their invariable response seemed to be a case of, "Oh well, I tried and failed; now I can just be friendly again," and they saw no reason why they or you should suddenly depart from one another's company. My presence, of course, provided an important safeguard; months later we met girls who told us that travelling through Asia was a totally different matter for a single female than for a couple.

• • •

Despite that one unsettling incident our time at Ürgüp was extremely laid-back and pleasant. When we regretfully decided it was time to depart we went by bus to nearby Nevşehir, fully intending to while away a few lazy hours there. However, we had hardly alighted from our vehicle when a man came dashing over, excitedly trying to tell us about some "great place you must see". He then dragged us across to a bus just then departing for this 'great place', making the driver wait as we climbed – or were pushed – on board. We felt as if a whirlwind had just overtaken us and we were stunned at how little control we had been able to exert over events. As the bus pulled out of the station the man ran alongside, waving and smiling up at us. We waved back, though somewhat automatically, still in a state of shock.

Our spontaneous tourist guide, however, had been perfectly correct in his assessment of this great place of his. The underground city of Derinkuyu, dug deep into the rocky terrain, was truly amazing. Descending the entrance shaft was like entering a beehive, with its narrow passageways leading ever onwards into a confusing – and frequently disconcerting – warren of interconnecting rooms. It is estimated that in this underground city – much of which has still to be excavated – 20,000 people may have lived on possibly as many as twenty levels. Not only had they hewn out living quarters, communal kitchens, ventilation and water shafts, but also wine presses, cellars, stables, a church and even cemeteries. Huge circular stone doors were used to seal the entrances, making the place impregnable to attack.

We had unfortunately resumed our travelling at an inappropriate time, for we both began to suffer from that inescapable travellers' ailment – diarrhoea. We blamed the midnight *sis kebab* meal but we could not be certain. What *was* certain was that it slowly began to drain our energy, which was already under assault from the debilitating heat. If that was not enough, one overnight stay was right beside a mosque – so much for our earlier intentions – and the greatly-amplified call to prayer in the early hours of the morning was ear-splitting. It really seemed as if the muezzin was standing in the room beside us.

In Adana we booked into a cheap hotel, purchased our tickets for onward travel, then went into the local public park to rest our weak legs and attempt to relax. It was a forlorn hope. Within minutes not only were we surrounded by a host of inquisitive, friendly faces but we were being engaged in a multitude of disparate conversations. One man we quickly established a rapport with, Turhan, whose wife was in hospital dying of cancer, introduced us to the members of the Atatürk Public Park Band and they duly formed their semicircle around our bench, and chatted, or plied us with coffee, or performed yet more beautiful *saz* music, letting us try our hand at playing the slender instrument.

Eventually we managed to bid our farewells to all these newfound friends and retired to our hotel room. Our intention was to rest for an hour then take a stroll through the neighbourhood. But as the evening wore on we found ourselves voicing different reasons for delaying our proposed walk, until we realised that these reasons were really excuses, and all occasioned by something we were loathe to admit – that we were hesitant to venture out in public again.

We realised that we desperately needed to be alone, to gain a respite from this deluge of human contact. This realisation was accompanied by a strong feeling of guilt, for, after all, what we were hiding from was the spontaneous hospitality of warm and generous people. But it had just been too much at times. To lessen our guilt we told ourselves that our hesitation resulted from our weak condition – but we knew that this was not the full story. Instead, we lay down on our beds, dabbed the sweat from our brows and tried to drift off into sleep.

Anyway, we needed that sleep, for the following day our journey east to Malatya proved to be long and tiring.

· · ·

As the bus approached, I automatically began to reach for my backpack, yet something about the vehicle perturbed me. Of course – it wasn't slowing down! I glanced quickly at Ercan but he just shrugged his shoulders, as mystified as we were. In astonishment I watched the bus from Ankara to Tatvan via Malatya drive straight past the bus station in Malatya without stopping! Was it full? Had we made a mistake?

Ercan smiled broadly.

"Well, you will have to stay with us now."

Ercan, who owned a workshop close to Malatya's central bus station, had befriended us the previous day when he had insisted upon taking us to his home to meet his lovely wife Mariam and their beautiful child Artem. Although we had tried to convince Ercan and Mariam that we were both still weak and only wished to eat a small amount, we were presented with a sumptuous feast which we did our best to consume, although I had to excuse myself frequently to visit the toilet and both our stomachs rumbled audibly all evening.

Not wanting to take a chance with another bus, we booked the train for early the next morning and Ercan announced that he was now taking us to his father's house. There we passed a beautifully relaxing day, much of it spent sitting in a quiet, shaded garden to the rear of the dwelling. Ercan's father was a handsome man with strong features who conversed with us in a patient and genuinely interested manner. At times his proud, almost patriarchal demeanour would briefly lapse – such as when I removed my contact lenses to clean them and he watched in almost childlike astonishment – but this only endeared him even more to us. Ercan and Mariam, despite our protestations, insisted they were going to sit up with us throughout the night and into the early hours of the morning. As our hosts plied us with food and refreshments we felt an initial guilt, for this was going far beyond a one-off gesture of hospitality and we had no means of reciprocating, but eventually we realised that our company – and our pleasure at *their* company – was reward enough for them. We felt very much at peace.

We would have relished that warm, peaceful atmosphere even more if we had known what lay just around the corner.

• • •

Tatvan was a shock.

For a start it was the dustiest place yet. But more importantly, for the first time in Turkey – leaving aside the incident at Ürgüp – we felt genuinely apprehensive. We had become accustomed to men staring, but to date those stares had been curious, benevolent. Here, however, as we walked along the main street, past long rows of solemn-faced men sitting outside çay shops, the stares behind the faces seemed malevolent, threatening. Children aggressively pursued us for money and when we ignored them they threw stones and taunted us with catcalls. In other parts of Turkey overzealousness on the part of children would have earned them a good clip around the ear from passing adults, but here, much to our dismay, the adults egged the youngsters on. To add to our concern, women would occasionally walk behind Sheila and then suddenly reach forward to nip her upper arms. There was no doubt about it – Tatvan was a shock.

Recoiling from our unfriendly reception in the town we walked to the outskirts in the hope of finding somewhere to camp well away from prying eyes, but there was nowhere, except for a deserted and derelict hotel/shopping complex, guarded by one ragged-dressed policeman – at least that is what he claimed to be. When he realised we were looking for somewhere to stay he broke into one of the better-kept of the buildings and asked if we would like to sleep there. However, we did not need intuition to tell us that such a move would have been highly unsafe, so we trudged wearily back into the town. Finally finding a room, we plonked ourselves down exhausted onto our beds and promptly fell asleep for five hours.

• • •

"This bloody useless backwater!"

The German paused and glared out over the shimmering waters of Lake Van.

"And I don't think there *is* a bloody boat!"

We had to agree with this last comment. The railway from Ankara ended here at Tatvan on the western end of the lake, and passengers travelling on to Iran had to cross the lake to Van on the eastern shore. Hoping to get tickets for this ferry we had walked out to the terminal, but what passed as a terminal was deserted and none of the occasional passers-by could give us the slightest information about the boat. The German pair had been stuck in Tatvan for two days and were now anxious to leave, by bus or by boat – whichever materialised first.

The German spoke disparagingly about the local people. In his opinion their aggressiveness probably derived from the fact that, as Kurds, they resented their lands being incorporated within the Turkish state and their antagonism towards Turks readily transferred itself onto all Westerners. He relayed some of the scare stories which had been circulating around the travellers' grapevine: alleged incidents of campers assaulted and drivers murdered.

We felt sad that eastern Turkey was living up to its negative reputation. We had been aware of it prior to our arrival, but had wanted to judge for ourselves and give the inhabitants of this region the benefit of the doubt. And we felt sad for these people; the depressed state of their circumstances would linger with us for a long time, more vivid than some of the scenes of dire poverty we would witness in India, for in India the outsider could still detect a resilience and an energy behind the poverty, whereas here the predominant image was one of resignation and apathy.

"What are you two going to do?"

"We'll stay another day. That mountain over there – Nemrut Daği, same name as the famous ruins far west of here – has a volcanic lake near its summit which is supposed to be very scenic. We'll probably take a walk up to it tomorrow."

The German expressed his doubts that anything in this "Godforsaken area" could be worth exploring.

"Well, best of luck; hope you have an interesting day."

It was certainly going to be just that!

• • •

"Look, just tell us one thing – are we under arrest or not!"

The army officer coughed embarrassedly, refusing to look us directly in the face.

"We are only detaining you. We . . ."

"But why!"

He wafted a fly away from his face and seemed relieved to hear the sound of the approaching staff car.

"We must check you are not spying for Greece."

At this comment, Sheila and I exchanged an anxious glance. The car halted beside us, the hum of the engine the only sound disturbing the stillness of the barren countryside. Waving a farewell to the crowd of gaping and smiling soldiers clustered at the fence which encircled their base we climbed into the back of the car. I turned to Sheila and forced a smile.

"At least it saves us walking back to town."

Taking surreptitious glances at us in his mirror the young soldier who was driving headed the car away from the camp and its overlooking mountain. I did not even bother to look back at it. Bloody nuisance of a mountain,

I muttered angrily. Our car arrived in Tatvan and proceeded to Turkish Army headquarters. We were directed to remain in the car, our driver now reassigned as our guard, until fifteen minutes later two more officers came out to the vehicle. What with the five officers we argued with back at the camp, I mused, we will soon be acquainted with their whole bleedin' general staff! They stared through the open window, frowning.

"Now, please tell us what you were doing near an army base."

And so, once again, I had to explain the circumstances which had led to our detention: our desire to visit the scenic lake on Nemrut Daği – indeed, it was our only reason for stopping off in Tatvan; the fact that people in the town, when we had asked which mountain it was, had pointed to the one we eventually climbed; the reasons we had not come down the same route we had ascended. The officer intervened:

"But you were not on Nemrut Daği."

"We know that now!"

In fact, we had known it some hours before, when, despite wearisome searching around the summit ridges, we could find no sign of a lake. Our irritation at having been seemingly directed to the wrong mountain had been exacerbated by the reception we had received from villagers on our approach walk. Children had thrown stones and grim-faced adults had advanced threateningly towards us, forcing us to beat a hasty retreat and then make an exhausting and needless detour. Indeed, perhaps this detour had caused us to lose our bearings; perhaps we had started out for the right mountain after all, but unwittingly climbed one nearby.

When we had lain down for a rest near the summit, still weak from our recent bout of stomach trouble and disheartened on discovering that the water in our bottles was hot and unpalatable, we had not relished the thought of returning past the village and so had decided to descend the mountain by a different route. But what a route! Whatever semblance of a goat path we thought we were following soon vanished and we were forced into a tortuous descent through tangled undergrowth, where distance gained seemed negligible and our exhaustion increased by the minute. At times the terrain was so steep we had to cling to the vegetation with our hands, and realising that to go back was now as difficult as continuing, our anxiety level rose dramatically.

But eventually the nightmare descent had ended and we reached level ground. Ahead of us a dirt-track weaved its way towards a long row of buildings and we proceeded along it, glad to be on ground which did not reach out tentacles to trip and delay. However, we had not gone far when we realised that the buildings constituted an army base, so once again we began to detour, as nonchalantly as we could.

Unfortunately, our presence had been noted and within minutes four fully-armed soldiers came running towards us, shouting out words which to us were unintelligible but whose meaning was perfectly clear. We halted and waited until the soldiers had surrounded us. We were then marched over to the perimeter fence and made to stand there, under guard, until an officer came sauntering over and began to question us. When he had finished he returned to the camp and five minutes later another officer came out. Then he too departed and yet another one came out . . . and another. What the hell was going on, I fumed anxiously – are they holding practice interrogations for their whole officer corps!

One officer had at least surprised us when scrutinising our passports. Like his colleagues his eyes narrowed when he saw our entrance stamp for Greece – possibly the root cause of our predicament. But this officer had noticed something else.

"Ah, you are from Belfast. Are you Catholic or Protestant?"

You can take your pick, I felt like saying, just as long as you let us go.

And now we were back in Tatvan, imprisoned in a stiflingly-hot car, with yet more officers peering through the open window. I again addressed the one who spoke good English.

"Look, when are we going to be released?"

"Not yet. The Commanding Officer was not at the camp to make a decision, that is why you were brought here. But he is not here either, so we must detain you until . . ."

I did not look at him any more, but pointedly lay back against the seat. So that was the reason – none of them were prepared to take responsibility for releasing us, even though they probably realised we were in fact only travellers.

The faces outside the window withdrew and Sheila and I exchanged exasperated glances. We attempted conversation with our driver/guard, but watchful eyes had witnessed this from across the courtyard, orders were barked and our companion was speedily replaced by another young soldier. Presumably this replacement cannot speak any English, I mused, though his predecessor had given no hint that he did either. How ludicrous can this get? I resigned myself to a long wait and tried to settle more comfortably into the seat. I looked again at Sheila and squeezed her hand; her face was creased with tension.

An agonisingly long time later the front passenger door snapped open, and, without so much as a glance at us, one of the officers got in and ordered the driver to proceed. This time our parking space was to be outside what seemed to be a joint army/police post, where a young policeman, with a more realistic appreciation of the true situation, came out to apologise, telling us that he himself had hitchhiked in Europe and knew we were not spies. He then muttered "But you know what soldiers are like", and told us that they had telephoned army headquarters in Izmir, close to where we had entered Turkey from Samos. As soon as the 'okay' came through, we would be released.

• • •

Four hours after we had first been apprehended we were the participants in an absurd open-air drama. The friendly policeman and the English-speaking army officer – plus obligatory driver – had taken us back to our hotel. Confirmation of our innocence had still not come through from Izmir, so it had been decided to place us under house arrest, with the hotel owner ordered to retain our passports until the all-clear was telephoned through to him.

That might have been the end of it, for we were weary and eager to see the back of Turkish army uniforms, but the officer, no doubt conscious of the large crowd of local people who had gathered around us on the pavement and were observing sullenly, took the opportunity to begin lecturing us in the most officious and condescending manner. This was simply the last straw for Sheila, on whom the four hours' detention – not to mention the exhausting climb and the aggressive villagers – had clearly taken its toll. She immediately launched into a verbal duel with the officer, and point for point vociferously matched his admonitions.

"If I was in your country I would not wander into an army base."

"We didn't wander *into* it! When we realised what it was we began to walk *around* it!"

"If I was in your country I would know not to even go close to an army base."

"That's because there'd be a big sign saying KEEP OUT – not like here!"

I was so engrossed in this remarkable bout that it was something of a shock to become suddenly aware that the sullen expressions on all those intently gathered around had vanished, to be replaced by an obvious glee. The officer now noticed it as well and his face blushed scarlet. If he had appeared condescending before, he looked furious now. The policeman seemed increasingly anxious and it dawned upon me what was transpiring. The local Kurdish people resented the presence of the Turkish army with a vengeance, and to see one of these spick and span officers receiving a public upbraiding from a foreigner – and a *female* foreigner to boot – was, for them, a scene to relish!

I realised that we had to cool things immediately or we could find ourselves in more trouble. However, Sheila must have had the same thought for she suddenly fell silent, while the officer, drawing himself up to full height, his face livid with anger, quickly turned on his heels and within seconds his car was erratically pushing its way through the jeering crowd.

Then, for the first time, the people of Tatvan were full of smiles for us and nods of approval were repeatedly directed towards Sheila, who now wore a sheepish look on her face rather than one of bravado. Any moment I expected to hear the sound of screeching vehicles as reinforcements arrived to drag us away again. The soothing voice of the policeman finally broke into my wild imaginings.

"Let me apologise again for all this, and let the police department treat you to a meal."

We looked at him appreciatively.

"It won't come out of your own pocket?"

"No, no; courtesy of the police department."

"Okay, then. But we must warn you – this has made us extremely hungry."

· · ·

The following day we sat on the deck of the ferry, in the company of its friendly captain, watching Tatvan recede into the distance. I held no grudge against the place, I reflected, but I could not say I was sorry to be leaving it. Then I remembered the captain's question and turned to him again.

"I can't think of any eligible girls back home, but when we return we'll put in a good word for you."

Captain Suphi Özavar laughed and slapped my knee. His face shone with a genuine and reassuring friendliness.

"Good, Michael, good! I like you both – you have good faces."

He then fell silent for a moment and seemed to become more serious.

"You see me: a well-off man, been a captain on different ships for ten years, my own boss. But am I satisfied? No, I would trade it all tomorrow for one loving wife, one welcoming home to come back to. Nothing is more important than that. And you, Michael, heed my words: your whole happiness is sitting right beside you; take care not to lose her."

Before we could reply he had leapt to his feet and signalled to one of the stewards.

"And now, my young travellers, you are to come down to my cabin for refreshments. And then, while I am tending to the ship, my cabin is completely at your disposal. If you wish to take a shower or if you have any clothes to wash there is plenty of hot water. Come!"

Sheila and I arose and followed him below decks, exchanging smiles with each other. Already the tension of Tatvan was evaporating. On the eve of exiting their country the hospitality of the Turkish people had once again reasserted itself. We just hoped that some day the good captain would be granted his wish.

Iran

(21–28 August 1976)

As our train neared the Iranian border the only other passengers in our compartment, two men who had already caused us concern because of their nervous fidgeting, now became increasingly agitated, and, most worrying of all, kept glancing apprehensively at the two large suitcases wedged into the luggage rack above our heads.

Finally, one of them leaned towards me and in a low, conspiratorial voice asked:

"Could you something do for us?"

I was taken aback and too full of instant suspicion to answer immediately.

"What do you mean?"

"We are carrying things we are not allowed to be bringing . . . in Iran. Please for me – would you put some in your . . . your bags for us."

I was dumbfounded and stared at him in disbelief. Did he think we were idiots! Not waiting for my reply the man jumped to his feet, hurriedly lumbered down one of the suitcases, set it precariously on his lap – I instinctively moved my own knees out of reach – and suddenly flipped open the lid. I do not know what I was expecting, but certainly not that which met my startled gaze – for the suitcase was bursting full of gaudy baubles: rings, necklaces, jewellery of all sorts.

"Please, I am trader, but I am not allowed to carry so much . . . so much goods. But if you carry some for me . . . then all is okay."

I looked at Sheila in alarm. Was this as innocent as it sounded? Now, on previous travels within Europe I had carried duty-free drink and cigarettes for fellow passengers – was this the local equivalent? Or could there be drugs secreted in those baubles? This part of our route abounded with stories of drug-smuggling and the penalties awaiting those caught. I scrutinised the large, pendulous earrings with deep suspicion.

"Please, I get trouble with police. I lose all my money. In your bags is good place."

He continued in this vein for some minutes until my head began to swim with the intensity of it all. Perhaps the man was simply trying to earn a bit more for his family. Perhaps splitting up merchandise among others was routine. But could we take such a risk? No-one would believe our side of the story if we were caught carrying hard drugs.

Then, my inner torment abruptly ceased, to be replaced by a cold resolve. The man had a problem, I told myself, but it was *his* problem, not ours. That was it – the matter had been decided, and I refused his request with a resoluteness that he must have realised would not weaken, for he sat back, crestfallen. Sheila and I were more than willing to help others in difficulty, but there could be no justification for taking such a risk.

When the Iranian customs officials eventually entered our compartment there was much arguing back and forth when they opened the two suitcases and eventually the men were escorted out, looking at me sorrowfully as they made their exit. I steeled myself against feeling any guilt. We could not afford to feel guilt, for even if this incident had been totally innocent, the next one might not be.

• • •

Teheran was not an immediately likeable place. Not that we had much opportunity to absorb the bustling street life, for our attention was constantly distracted by the incessant intrusion of the city's cars, the majority of them taxis. As we walked through the streets a taxi would cruise alongside, the driver shouting and beckoning to us and all the while sounding his horn to a persistent and irritating tempo. When he eventually accepted that we were not interested in availing of his services and sped away, it was only to be replaced by another taxi and the calling and the honking would resume, without any noticeable intermission.

The honking was not reserved solely for us, of course, but seemed to be an obligatory component of driving in this city. And the supposed 'pedestrian crossings' were a mockery – crossing the road in Teheran was by far the closest we had ever come to engaging in an extreme contact sport.

But while the taxi-drivers eagerly sought our custom, it was not so with some shopkeepers. In three different shops, as we waited to be served, the owners pointedly ignored us, served the next person in line, and we had no option but to leave empty-handed. The staff in the tourist information office at least spoke to us, but were just as unhelpful. It was such a contrast with Turkey and so confusing. Part of us wanted to give the city a try, part of us said 'why bother?' In the end, the 'why bother' won out – and we bought tickets for the 9.30pm bus to Esfahan.

·   ·   ·

For a place reputed to be 'one of the most beautiful cities in Asia', we thought that Esfahan, at first sight, might have difficulty living up to such an accolade. Admittedly, the extremely long walk to the supposed youth hostel had taken us through grubby and grimy areas typical of all major urban environments. Perhaps the intense heat also coloured our assessment, plus the shock of discovering how expensive everything was – even the fee for camping in the hostel grounds took us aback. We doubted whether we could afford to spend three weeks in Iran as originally intended.

The following day Esfahan had greatly improved! It is amazing what a restful sleep and a full stomach can do for a city's appearance. We told ourselves to bear in mind from now on that backpackers invariably saw the most rundown parts of a city *before* they saw the better parts. Arriving by train, bus or boat, they often had to trudge wearily through congested commercial sectors, or the less-affluent parts where cheap accommodation would more readily be located. If in such areas a bustling and colourful street life predominated then the grubbiness could be overlooked. If, however, it was the dust and grime which registered most on the senses, then the first – and often lasting – impression was negative.

But tucked away inside Esfahan-the-modern-urban-sprawl lay Esfahan-the-jewel. Its mosques were some of the finest examples of Persian Islamic architecture and art. Every square inch of the Royal Mosque, or Masjid-i-Shah, for example, was adorned with multicoloured light-reflecting tilework, and was a veritable 'rhapsody in blue', that being the predominant colour. Although some of the city's monuments dated back to the 11th Century,

43

most – as with the great squares and avenues – were constructed in the early 17th Century when Esfahan became the opulent capital of the Safavid kings of Persia. We sat for a long time by the pool in the central courtyard of the Masjid-i-Shah, mesmerised by the beautiful and highly intricate floral and geometric motifs with which craftsmen had managed to fill every conceivable bit of space on the surrounding walls, and all done with a dazzling exactitude and profusion of design.

Just as intriguing, and far more bustling and lively, was the great covered bazaar, in which entire sections were devoted to separate crafts: pottery, carpets, metalwork, textiles, miniature paintings – a veritable treasure trove into which we immersed ourselves for hours.

• • •

But for the traveller, the exultation – whether momentary or lingering – which is felt at any new discovery, any enthralling experience, must be balanced with purely logistical concerns and mundane realities. The question of climate, for example: if we followed our intended itinerary and travelled further south in Iran, could we cope with the intense heat? Then the question of finances: could we actually afford to linger in Iran, when we had so much more ground to cover? And now politics: could we even *get* south?

For we had been told that the Shah of Iran would be travelling in a few days' time to our next intended destination, the southern city of Shiraz, for yet another ceremony extolling his grandeur. The problem for us was that he would be travelling with a large retinue, one which – so our informant insisted – would effectively close the roads. Not a retinue ordained solely by the pomp and circumstance befitting the inheritor of the Peacock Throne, but one also necessitated by the security needs of a ruler increasingly at odds with his own people. Indeed, we were assured that the cold-shouldering we and other Westerners received was mainly a reflection of the widespread detestation which existed for the Westernisation the Shah and his family were trying to impose.

And so we weighed up all these factors and decided that it was perhaps prudent to leave Iran. Less than three years later the Shah himself was to come to the same conclusion.

· · ·

Upon our return to Teheran we were walking through the city centre when a young man abruptly stepped in front of us.

"I welcome you to my country. I hope you have a good time."

As suddenly as he had approached us he disappeared again into the crowd. Yet in our brief encounter we had made eye contact, and I felt certain I had gleaned a hint of his purpose. It was as if he wanted to make personal amends for any slights caused by his compatriots.

Some years later we would meet other travellers who had crossed Iran while it was in the throes of revolution and had found that much of the resentment towards travellers was gone. The antagonism to most things Western was still there, indeed it was being vociferously expressed, but the people had regained their sense of pride: they were able to welcome travellers to *their* country, not one fabricated by their monarch in a Western image.

At the bus station we purchased tickets for Mashad. The bus was to leave at 8am and as there was little point in searching out a hotel we settled down to sleep in the station. The police, however, insisted that we go outside where, in the company of a few other travellers, we lay ourselves down upon the pavement.

The journey to Mashad took an exhausting twenty hours, and after a brief rest there we boarded another bus bound for the Afghan border.

Afghanistan
(28 August – 16 September 1976)

Herat, a few hours drive by minibus into Afghanistan, was a beautiful place. Not necessarily beautiful in a physical sense, for weary travellers often have other categories in mind when they award such a commendation. For a start, it was restful – gone were the noisy taxis of Turkey and Iran and in their place were bicycles and horse-drawn tongas replete with sheltering hoods and festooned with red pompons. As well as that, the Afghan men looked wonderfully exotic in their turbans and baggy trousers, though not nearly as exotic as the manner in which lorries and buses had been painstakingly and extravagantly decorated. The pace of life seemed slower too, almost deliberately relaxed; certainly we could not imagine these people emulating the near-frenzied bustle we had witnessed elsewhere. And while the food shops were sparse in their merchandise, nourishing items such as melon, honey, yoghurt and bread were all readily available. We would stand mesmerised outside the open-fronted bakeries to watch the whole process take place in minutes, and the hot unleavened bread tasted unbelievably good and filling. As I said, travellers have their own criteria as to what makes a place appear beautiful.

We needed no coaxing to relax in Herat, even allowing ourselves to buy some hash – after all, we *were* following the Hippie Trail. However, we were so naturally high in our new surroundings that our token purchase sat on a shelf in our lodgings, untested, unneeded.

On arrival in the town we had booked into a cheap hotel but soon hurriedly vacated our room to erect our tent, with great difficulty, in the stony courtyard, fleeing our first real encounter with bedbugs. We had wearily plonked ourselves down onto our beds upon entering the room, only to jump up in alarm a few minutes later when we realised that the mattresses were infested.

The only abnormality about the town was the near-absence of women on the streets; any who did make an appearance were invisible behind the chador with its pitifully small visor. A friendly young tailor's assistant – the only reasonably fluent English speaker we encountered – painted a depressing picture of the lot of Afghan women. He summed it up by describing his own sister's story: married at sixteen, had ten children (five of whom died) and now looked forty instead of twenty-six.

We had visited the tailor's to be measured for a set of Afghan clothes each, for although the European clothes we possessed might have been hard-wearing, they were hot – very hot. Our measurements were carefully taken, to be duly passed on to the tailor, who would have the garments ready for collection the following day. However, as the young assistant put down his tape-measure and began writing, a deep frown creased his forehead.

"Is there a problem?"

"No, no – no problem."

But there *was* a problem, although we were not to discover it until the following day. When we arrived back at the shop our young friend seemed embarrassed about something, and even before he handed us our new garments profuse apologies were tumbling forth.

"I am sorry, I am sorry. I knew he would not believe me."

"Believe you about what?"

"Your measurements. He said I must have got them wrong. So, I am afraid that . . ."

He scrutinized my 6' 4" height and shook his head yet again.

". . . the legs will be a little short."

I smiled to reassure him. The legs were indeed a little short, but – who cared?

• • •

The main road through Afghanistan – going west to east – swings south through the city of Kandahar. However, we were more intrigued by the possibility of an alternative northern route via Mazar-i-Sharif. As this route ran close to the border with the USSR, all foreigners were required to obtain police permits, and these we duly set out to acquire. This quest entailed a minor trek in its own right – from one office to another, and then back to

47

ones already visited. There was no hassle, no hint that we were pursuing an illusory objective – on the contrary, it was all done with smiles and a well-practised lack of urgency. It was fascinating to watch our permits – which resembled overly ornate examination certificates – being gradually filled up with each office's authorisation, entered in beautiful swirling handwriting by professional scribes. Not only that, but for some reason each separate entry was done in a different colour. I looked at the completed document with admiration, already visualising it as a treasured memento framed on a wall back home.

The northern route was just that – a route rather than a road – and could only be undertaken in large open jeeps, known as 'Russian buses', a reference to their country of origin. The robust construction of these vehicles made them particularly suitable for the type of terrain which lay ahead. The journey to Mazar-i-Sharif was accomplished in separate stages, and as we set forth on the first stage, to Quala Nau, wedged tightly between our fellow passengers, we had hardly travelled far when our vehicle stopped at a police post where we were asked to hand over our precious permits. A policeman gave them a cursory glance and then waved the driver on.

"What about our permits?"

"Is okay, you go. No need. Is okay now."

"But I want to keep them!"

"Is okay, you go. Goodbye."

There was nothing I could do, and as the police post receded behind us I looked at Sheila and shrugged my shoulders. She just smiled and tried to settle more comfortably against the side of the vehicle. An amazing journey had just begun.

• • •

The truck lurched violently over another rough stretch, causing the old man to again lose hold of his turban, and it quickly unravelled itself, streaming out behind us in the wind. He muttered angrily, the other passengers responding with more shrills of laughter and mischievous banter. And we laughed with them, for their laughter was warm, and the old man was left no choice but to smile ruefully – a clownish, toothless smile – and try again. This time two pairs of hands came to his aid and the task was successfully accomplished, he himself adding the finishing touch by passing the free end across his mouth and tucking it into the folds above his head.

I blinked painfully as more dust found its way into my left eye. I could use a shielding turban myself, I moaned. Another blast of dust and grit hit us as the truck hurtled onwards. Both eyes now began to smart painfully. Damn it, I moaned, I'll have to do something quickly. I glanced around at the faces peering intently at me from behind their turban folds. They had been watching me thoughtfully for some time now, probably wondering why this foreigner was constantly fidgeting with his eyelids. Well, this should intrigue them, I mused.

Smiling apologetically to my immediate fellow-passengers, I reached over their legs and gripped the harness of my backpack. At first it wouldn't budge, but finally it wrenched free from the vice-like grip of baskets and bedding, frightening the chickens into such a state that my shoes were liberally decorated. I returned a rueful smile with the youth opposite. And then all the private conversations lapsed into a hush as I unearthed a small container and a pair of spectacles from the depths of my backpack and proceeded to remove my contact lenses. As I gingerly placed each lens into the container the other passengers somehow managed to extricate themselves from previously immovable positions and leaned forward, faces intent and perplexed.

Luckily our travelling companions did not ask to hold one of the lenses, for the wind would have whipped it away in seconds. Our watches and Sheila's wedding ring had already been passed from one to the other several times, the wedding ring having the additional privilege of reassuring them, for here, as in other Asian countries, you could feel a palpable tenseness until they ascertained that you were 'man and wife', and then previously worried faces would relax into warm smiles.

• • •

And so we progressed across northern Afghanistan, reaching Quala Nau the first day, Bala Murghab the second, Maimana the third, changing jeeps and meeting new travelling companions on each stage, and sleeping at nights on the floors of dusty, desolate, dimly-lit buildings which served as travellers' lodgings. We assumed that the drivers knew the route by instinct, for at times we could see no indication whatsoever of any track.

Sometimes the gradient would cause the jeep to slow to a halt and we would all pile out, to follow the unladen vehicle up the slope, our feet sinking into dust a foot deep. Other times we would dismount for the opposite reason – when the descent was so steep a laden jeep could have careered downhill out of control over the loose surface. On the 'safer' occasions the drivers would often indicate that we – as special passengers – could remain on board, but as these breaks were the only opportunity we got to take photographs, we always dismounted with the others, hoping each time that we would be near one of the numerous camel caravans or at least in a good position to capture some of the magnificent and starkly rugged scenery.

While travelling on one particular jeep it was during such a dismount that I had first taken our camera from its protective concealment, and when we resumed our journey obvious references were made to it. A few minutes later the jeep halted on the brow of a hill and everyone – the men, that is, for the women did not like being photographed – piled out anew to pose for a group photograph, not exactly in the way I would have liked but in one long line which sent me clambering up the hillside so as to fit everyone into the viewfinder. Then the driver and co-driver insisted on a photograph with only themselves in it, then two more posed together, and to conserve film I had to make a clicking sound and hope that it sounded convincingly like a camera shutter.

Our hair was so matted our comb broke in two and our clothes were caked with dust and sand, but we both felt exhilarated. What a country! What a people! These unassuming villagers exuded an infectious friendliness and ten minutes after getting into any jeep we felt we had known our fellow passengers for weeks. Beautiful bass and tenor voices would serenade us almost continuously with harmonious folk songs, often accompanied on a home-made instrument not unlike the Turkish *saz*.

There was one moment of sourness, however. On the third day two other European backpackers joined our jeep for part of the journey. As we sat squeezed into our positions, with those on one side of the vehicle staring into the faces of those opposite, one of the newcomers began to photograph the women. There was no permission sought, no friendly overtures made.

The women endeavoured to look away, clearly highly embarrassed, while the menfolk could barely conceal their anger, and I am convinced that it was only their innate hospitality which held them back from going for the two men. In fact, it was I who proved unable to contain myself.

"I don't think the women like being photographed."

"That's too bad!"

I was taken aback by this arrogance.

"You could at least have asked them."

"They probably would have said 'no'. I didn't come all this bloody way not to be able to take whatever photographs I want!"

Bastard, I thought, what an ignorant bastard!

The incident soured the rest of that particular journey and the gaiety of our Afghan fellow-passengers abruptly ceased. For the sake of a couple of photographs these two selfish travellers had not only killed any spontaneity but sown a simmering resentment. I tried by non-verbal means to convey to the other passengers how much we disliked what had transpired but I am not sure whether I was successful. We were glad to see the back of the pair when we eventually parted company.

•　•　•

Ahead of us another cluster of simply constructed mud-brick houses loomed up amid the barrenness and yet more passengers and their luggage somehow got squeezed on board. One was a soldier dressed in the tattered and patched uniform which was apparently the hand-me-down garment issued to those doing their compulsory stint. Here, for once, a military uniform imparted none of the customary aloofness to its owner, and the soldier, the possessor of an excellent voice, led the singing. Some of the newcomers munched away at food, which we thought strange considering that this was the Muslim fasting period of Ramadan during which no-one was supposed to eat between sunrise and sunset. It was explained to us that travellers were exempt, though most of those we met did not avail themselves of this dispensation. The fast assisted us, however, as it meant we were not alone in politely refusing to drink from the oilcans which were frequently passed around, containing 'drinking' water filled directly from murky streams.

On the fourth day of our jeep journey the town of Shibarghan was finally in sight, and with two other jeeps having joined us and now competing for a dust-free front position on the single track, our driver suddenly branched off and sped, at an exhilarating pace, across the open desert. Soon the other jeeps followed suit and we arrived at our destination more in the manner of the Long Range Desert Group attacking a supply base than the local public transport delivering its passengers. From here to Mazar-i-Sharif the road was surfaced – our desert jeep-trek was over.

• • •

The mosque and mausoleum at Mazar-i-Sharif was built to honour Mohammed's son-in-law, Ali, one of the Prophet's successors. Muslims dispute Ali's burial place: some believe he lies entombed near Al Kufah in Iraq, others that his body lies here at Mazar-i-Sharif – the name means 'tomb of the saint'. Indeed, to ensure paying their respects, some pilgrims visit both sites. We were not permitted to enter beyond the perimeter railing but at least we could admire the magnificent exterior of the building. Islam forbids the representation of the human form on religious buildings, and, by way of compensation, Islamic craftsmen and artists have developed the skills of calligraphy and ornamentation into the highest art forms. And here, on the façade of this great mosque, that artistry was very much in evidence.

We had supposed that Mazar-i-Sharif might have been a good place to rest up after our desert jeep-trek, but – apart from the beautiful mosque – the town with its sprawl of poverty and dirt held little to detain us, and after a day's rest and a good scrub we were anxious to be on our way again.

• • •

It is hard to find adequate words to describe the sight which met our eyes as our bus began its descent of the mountainside. In the valley below, set within an arid and barren landscape enclosed by rugged cliffs, lay a string of sparkling jewels: the lakes of Band-i-Amir. During the course of our travels many scenic wonders would remain indelibly imprinted on our memories, but some would stand out in a class of their own, and at the top of the class-list would be Band-i-Amir. These lakes alone would justify travelling halfway across Asia.

In such a scorchingly hot setting, where water was the last thing you expected to encounter, the first sight of the lakes is quite startling. Fed by meltwater carried down from the mountain peaks in the spring, the six lakes are held in place behind natural dams created when deposits of calcium carbonate hardened into a semitranslucent travertine. And the colours of the lakes – milky white, azure, turquoise, blue and green – are made more intense by being positioned between a cloudless blue sky and a golden desert landscape.

Our bus, on which we had travelled some fifty gruelling miles from the quiet village of Bamian – where we had visited two massive 6th Century statues of the Buddha carved out of the cliffside – deposited us at a small makeshift settlement which was, in its own way, just as startling to find here as were the lakes. Rudimentary dwellings, topped with shade-providing awnings, sported banners with notices such as EVERY THINGS ARE READY FOR YOUR SHOPPING and BEDROOMS HERE ALSO. Some of these 'bedrooms' were nothing more than an area of carpet under an awning with enough space to lay out a few sleeping-bags, while others were more substantial. This small settlement seemed to exist primarily to cater for backpackers.

The hippies of the 1960s had found themselves sharing the route to India with an assortment of backpackers who were venturing forth not from any esoteric imperative but simply lured by the adventure of travelling. Now, in the mid-1970s, backpackers like ourselves far outnumbered any hippie contingent. And all along the Hippie Trail many places had witnessed the blossoming of budget accommodation, pie-shops, beach restaurants and the like. Often the entrepreneurs behind these small-scale developments were local people trying to augment a basic living, and they and their easy-going customers managed to meet each other's needs in a way which did not spoil or abuse the surrounding environment. Such as here at Band-i-Amir, where the makeshift facilities made the lake area accessible to backpackers without destroying its tranquillity and solitude in the process.

The few days we spent at Band-i-Amir were days of enchantment and wonder. Despite the intense heat we went for long leisurely walks around the lakes and even attempted to paddle in the shallow pools where one lake fed into another – only to retreat in astonishment upon discovering that even in these pools the water was bitterly cold. The area was not as uninhabited as it had first appeared, and there was a village nearby where we bought food and whose women were not averse to being photographed. These women were also the first Afghan women we had encountered to reveal their faces, and looked – and probably were, given the history of the area's invaders – of Mongol descent.

• • •

The bus had taken us on board at 6am – the stated departure time – and driven to the outskirts of Bamian, en route for Kabul, or so we thought. But no, near the limit of the inhabited area it turned and drove back to the opposite end of the town, the co-driver leaning from the cab and striving to attract more custom. Once again it set forth in the direction of Kabul and once again it returned. A third attempt to leave Bamian took us right to the outskirts and a stop for fuel. Good, we thought, hopefully this is a sign that we will soon be on our way. But it was not to be. The petrol pump's indicator was not functioning and the driver obviously disagreed with the attendant's estimate of his vehicle's consumption, for a heated argument erupted which soon attracted a large crowd. We shook our heads and watched it all from our ringside seats. We knew what to expect, for in some strange way these verbal confrontations – and they were frequent – rarely threatened to deteriorate into physical violence, although an obligatory period of time had to pass before each participant could withdraw without loss of face.

Eventually we did leave the outskirts of Bamian, merely to halt a short distance later, this time waiting while a nomad family not only bundled its entire worldly possessions on board – hens included – but dismantled its huge black awning of a tent, piece by piece. Surely there cannot be room for all this, we thought. But somehow there was, and just when we had come to believe that we could not be squeezed any tighter, we were proven wrong.

Finally at 8am the bus did set off, some passengers riding on the roof amid the luggage. It was these upper-deck travellers who caused the next stoppage. Normally when approaching a police post rooftop passengers descend and squeeze inside, resuming their former places after the police-post has fallen from sight. This time, however, on arrival in a small village, the driver, for some reason which we never understood, ordered them all off the bus completely – perhaps he had only agreed to a free lift to this village. They pointedly refused, and with growing incomprehension we watched our furious driver storm angrily down the road!

Other passengers took charge, some climbing up on top to insist that those perched there descend, while others ran to pacify the driver, a task which, of course, required the obligatory period of time. The driver had no sooner regained the wheel when a large hen, excited no doubt by all the commotion, jumped from the bus. Aided, or perhaps hindered, by gleeful yells from the bus passengers and the assembled throng of villagers, half a dozen youths chased the terrified creature through a hedge, across a field and into a stream before finally retrieving it, dumping the bedraggled specimen unceremoniously on the floor of the vehicle.

Once or twice the vehicle stopped far from any sign of habitation, and when none of the passengers used the opportunity to dismount and attend to their prayers – the usual reason behind such halts – we would scan our surroundings expectantly. Finally, seemingly materialising out of nowhere, figures would slowly make their way towards us, and we realised that we were parked at a desert bus-stop. The driver would not think of shortening the waiting time by driving over to meet his new customers, but sat patiently until everyone was aboard.

At one point the bus had to be completely evacuated after trying to drive past a truck on a narrow stretch of road with the result that the two vehicles became jammed together. Road travel was by far the most dangerous part of the overland trip – with many vehicles being driven with a reckless and terrifying abandon – yet one rule every driver did generally comply with was that the vehicle coming *uphill* always had right of way. Perhaps the drivers appreciated the precarious mechanical condition of each other's vehicles and the problems there could be if a stall occurred while making an ascent. Without hesitation, therefore, drivers would endeavour to create a clear passage for vehicles approaching uphill. However, it was a different matter when two vehicles approached one another on level ground – then there was no quarter given, which is what had transpired in this instance.

Of course, the two drivers had to engage in another protracted argument, participated in by some of the passengers, while others took the opportunity to stretch their legs or sit in small groups chatting. Finally all the men rocked the lighter of the two vehicles back and forth until it had freed itself from the other's grip.

Eventually we did reach Kabul, cramped but relieved and itching all over from insect bites.

• • •

We were informed by other backpackers that Kabul had been nicknamed the 'city of dysentery' – not the most reassuring information to hear upon arrival in the Afghan capital. Yet, despite all the scare stories passing around the traveller's grapevine, we needed to rest up for a few days, to let us recuperate from all our recent bus journeys, for while they had been exhilarating they had also been exhausting. We did not even try to ascertain what historical sights Kabul might have to offer and contented ourselves with walking up and down 'Chicken Street' – the hippie haunt – dropping into a cake shop more than occasionally. We smoked a little of our Herat hash, then gave the bulk of it away to a spaced-out fellow traveller. We realised we had little need for such escapism when our days were filled to the brim with so many new experiences, and each waking hour was being lived to its fullest.

Walking around the streets we were again amazed at how many street children and young people in Asia could converse in different foreign languages. And for many this was not simply a case of knowing basic nouns and verbs – "You go to hotel?" – but all the connecting tenses as well – "Are you looking for a room? I will take you to a good one." As this fluency had been acquired on the streets, not in the classroom, it was obvious that the imperative to survive and make a living was an excellent incentive to learning. Everywhere young people would approach travellers offering to act as guides, or to take them to hotels, or to transport them about on trishaws. One situation we encountered epitomised the adaptability of these young people.

Because travelling in Asia necessitated lengthy waits for trains and buses, even longer journeys, and numerous evenings sitting quietly outside your lodgings – or inside if the local mosquitos were active – one of the most valuable commodities to acquire was a good book. Indeed, often the first words exchanged when backpackers met were "Any books to swap?" A good *thick* book, one which you hoped would last for ages. Because of this requirement two of the most sought-after authors were James Mitchener and Leon Uris. Anyway, as we were perusing market stalls in the Chicken Street area, we came upon one displaying second-hand English paperbacks, the stall-holder a youth of perhaps fourteen. This young entrepreneur had his books priced according to thickness, except for one – a thin title by Hermann Hesse. I lifted it up and pointed to the ranks of slim books.

"Is this not the same price as these ones?"

"No, no – it is same price as these ones here."

For comparison I held the thin volume against one of the thicker books he had indicated.

"But it is much smaller than them."

The youth looked at me as if I was severely deficient in my education.

"Ah," he said rather dramatically, "but this one is by Hermann Hesse!"

Hesse, the poet of the inner journey, the spiritual guide for those journeying to the East – the youth certainly knew his merchandise and his customers!

• • •

I made my way slowly back to where Sheila waited hopefully, but her face fell when she observed my glum look.

"There's no two ways about it – our rucksacks are gone."

As anxiety began to cloud her features, I cast my eyes around, struggling to think of what we could do now.

"There's a Post Office opposite – maybe we could telephone the border police."

We hurried over to the building and proceeded purposefully to the counter.

"Excuse me – have you a telephone here?"

The staff exchanged looks with us, then with each other, then with us again, but no-one moved.

"Telephone? Have you a tel-e-phone? Please."

More looks were exchanged then one youth jumped to his feet and exited the room. I turned to Sheila and raised my eyebrows, but we suspected what was taking place and waited patiently. A few seconds later the youth returned, followed more sedately by an older man. This older man approached the counter, then nodded courteously and smiled. To our relief, when he spoke it was in perfect English.

"Hello. Can I help you?"

"Thank you for coming out to see us. We have a problem. We got on a bus in Kabul going to the Pakistan border, and when it stopped here in Jalalabad the driver told us to go and eat, and he would resume the journey in thirty minutes."

"Yes?"

"Well, the bus, with our luggage on board, then drove away – we thought the driver was also going to find somewhere to eat – but did not return. And an hour and a half has now passed."

The man scrutinised us up and down, probably not sure what to make of us let alone our problem. His face was such a picture of seriousness we imagined it likely put on for the benefit of the other staff, whose eyes were all riveted upon our little gathering.

"The bus left you off out there?" He pointed to the line of buses across the street.

"Yes. Right outside."

"Well, the bus from Kabul stops here, yes – for this is the arrival and departure point for Kabul. But buses going to the border depart from a completely different place – ten minutes walk towards the other side of town. He would have gone there to pick up more passengers."

We shook our heads in amazement. Why had the driver not come back when he found us missing? More to the point, why had he not informed us about the different departure point?

"I think it best you take a minibus to the border. You may find he has left your luggage there."

"We'll do that. Thank you very much for your help."

Striding quickly past the lines of road-stalls, much to the amusement of other pedestrians, we soon reached the 'border bus-stop' and squeezed into a waiting minibus, just moments before it departed for the border. How strange it felt not to be fumbling and straining over our backpacks!

One youth seated near us was observant enough to sense our unease and in a comical exchange of half-understood English he was soon acquainted with our predicament. He grinned broadly, showing an equal mixture of black and yellow teeth.

"Our buses . . . not so good, yes?"

Not so good, perhaps, but never uninteresting.

Sheila and I pressed our faces against the windows, scanning the line of vehicles returning from the border. Eventually Sheila nudged me.

"Is that it?"

I peered hard ahead. With all the lorries and buses being individually painted and decorated, even the coachwork being different, it was impossible to remember exactly what special characteristics a particular vehicle possessed.

"No, I don't think so. Ours didn't have those curved railings on top. Don't worry, at least it must still be somewhere ahead of us."

A few more miles and Sheila suddenly nudged me again, this time with greater urgency.

"That's it! I'm sure of it!"

It was. I leaned between the passengers in front and tapped our driver on the shoulder, gesticulating at the approaching bus. To my consternation he did not comprehend and while the youth quickly came to our aid and endeavoured to explain, I stuck my head out through the window and waved frantically. To our great relief the two vehicles came to a halt a few dozen yards apart and the minibus reversed to where our backpacks were already being lowered down to the ground. When the reason for our joyous expressions became clear to the passengers on both vehicles they broke into grins and laughter. With our belongings in our possession once more and our minds at rest, we set off again for the border.

• • •

"Do you have any money to change?"

I stared at the Afghan police officer as he returned our passports, not sure how to respond to his question.

"Why . . . yes, we have. Is there . . . a bank near?"

He laughed and rose from his desk.

"Don't go to bank. We give better rate. How much you want to change?"

My hesitation must have been only too apparent, though he obviously misunderstood its origin.

"It's okay, not worry – we give proper black market rate."

Still with a vague feeling that this could be a trick, I handed over our surplus Afghan money. Counting it quickly the policeman proceeded to the door, where, pausing momentarily to give a surreptitious glance around, he made his way smartly to the rear of the building. Sheila and I stared at each other and then burst out laughing. We were still laughing when he returned and pressed Pakistani banknotes into my palm.

"I take it we don't . . . declare this?"

"No, no. Hide it in your pocket. Not worry, they not search Westerners."

And nor did they. Anyway, before we could even reach the Pakistan border-post we had to fight our way past pestering Pakistani money-changers openly flaunting thick wads of money. We laughed again at the absurdity of it all.

Pakistan
(16–27 September 1976)

The Khyber Pass, despite its romantic history, was not all that inspiring and as our vehicle traversed it we felt a little disappointed. The border town of Landi Kotal too was a packed, grubby place with offers of hash coming at us from every quarter. Even the sight of so many gun-toting men held no fascination, for our travels were in part an escape from an Ireland where the bloody reality of the 'armed struggle' had killed any possible romance which could possibly be attached to a gun culture. The road to Peshawar seemed to contain its own dangers – since Jalalabad we had actually witnessed two crashes and driven past the aftermath of three more. Peshawar itself, with huge buzzards constantly circling overhead, seemed a dirty, sprawling place, a first impression not helped by the fact that our cheap hotel was tucked away behind a large motor yard. If that was not enough, we had been caught in our first torrential rainstorm since arriving in Asia – a welcome enough respite in different circumstances, but not when you are trudging around with backpacks. The one saving grace was the friendliness of the people, and we trusted that all the negative impressions would, as so often before, vanish with another dawn.

• • •

As our bus strained along the road which was taking us ever higher into the mountains, I should have felt at ease, for mountains were our favourite terrain. Yet two major concerns were playing on my mind. The first was that our journey held all the potential of being a real cliffhanger – literally. We had already encountered one overturned vehicle perched precariously on the edge of the road, and had been informed by those gathered around it that six rooftop passengers had been catapulted to their deaths into the ravine below. Nearly every corner was a blind corner and we never knew whether a descending vehicle would come careering around it, or what condition the edge of the road would be in.

The second concern was that stomach trouble had again caught up with me. The queasiness I had experienced on other occasions, however, paled into insignificance when compared to the burning turbulence which was now afflicting my insides. And to have an incredibly smelly goat wedged beside us in the aisle hardly helped matters. Indeed, as we progressed deeper into the beautiful Swat valley, in Pakistan's North-West Frontier Province, I had to leap from two separate vehicles – while they momentarily halted at obstacles – and dash into the undergrowth, much to the consternation of the drivers. Meanwhile Sheila endeavoured to explain to them that I was not running away and would definitely be coming back.

But eventually, at the end of the motorable road, we reached the small town of Kalam, relieved to know that we would be resting up for a few days. We found a homely and inexpensive hillside hotel, where we got a room which not only had an attached bathroom but actually boasted a double bed – up until now a 'double room' in Asia had invariably meant a room containing two single beds. Our room had an outside veranda overlooking the Swat river and for a while we sat watching the last rays of the sun go down across the surrounding valley. That evening we had a meal in a kitchen so dark its single oil lamp barely made an impression, and watched the friendly staff inhale hashish through straws after putting water in their mouths. Despite my physical weakness we felt relaxed and contented. It was nice to fall asleep in each other's arms again, at peace and alone. At least we thought we were alone.

• • •

"That's sixty-one. No, there's another one behind your ankle – that makes sixty-two."

It was hard to inject any levity into what I was doing, especially as I was feeling so guilty at Sheila's condition. She observed me with a pained expression.

"How come you've hardly got any?"

"I don't know. Maybe they don't go for me; maybe they don't like the taste of my blood; maybe they do bite me but my skin doesn't react the same way as yours."

It was indeed a mystery. This was not the first occasion Sheila had been bitten by bedbugs while I had been left relatively unmolested, but we had always assumed that she was just unlucky to have picked the wrong bed. Even when I would thoroughly inspect the beds and lie down on them to see what might emerge – prepared to take the most 'alive' one – she always ended up with far more bites than I. But now, for the first time in ages, we had slept in the *same* bed, and I had *still* been mostly unaffected, while she sported sixty-two assorted bites.

For a while we searched out the blighters and exacted our revenge by cracking them between our thumbnails, but with each splattering of blood we gradually lost interest and finally desisted. Despite the scale of Sheila's latest suffering, at least our attitude was just to bear with it and not let it worry us – there was no repeat of the doubts experienced in Yugoslavia.

Getting out for walks was the best remedy and Kalam was an ideal place for that. After a filling breakfast of Swat honey and bread, we would set off on long leisurely hikes, including an eight-hour easy trek to the source of the Ushu river and back. Not only were the mountain vistas beautiful – particularly the glimpses of Mount Falakser – but the people we met were friendly and generous. Everyone was out collecting walnuts and no-one would pass us without pressing nuts and assorted fruit into our hands.

At one village where festivities were in progress laughing children insisted I pick up a gun and take pot-shots at tethered balloons, showing their delight when I repeatedly scored direct hits. A few local men, bandoleers across their chests and rifles cradled proudly in their arms, came over and nodded approvingly.

"Good, good! They shoot good in your country?"

How could you answer that?

• • •

As we sat by the riverbank the local obsession with carrying guns gave me cause for reflection. When the initial hopes of the Northern Ireland Civil Rights movement – in which we had both participated – crumbled between the pincers of a resurgent Irish Republicanism and a reactionary Ulster Loyalism, I had endeavoured to add my own efforts to those who were attempting to halt the escalating violence. But while the uninvolved middle class could pontificate with ease, those working at the grassroots found any centre-ground being inexorably squeezed. My first threat emanated from the Loyalist camp, for whom any 'Protestant' Civil Rights agitator was deemed a traitor. Two men had stepped out in front of me as I walked along the street:

"We're gonna get you, you bastard! Just wait and see!"

Then, when I published a document which not only castigated the sectarianism of the Northern Ireland state but the IRA's indiscriminate bombing campaign, a 'message' from members of the Provisional IRA was passed through an intermediary:

"Tell yer mate that if he writes stuff like that again, he'll get his knees ventilated."

When I reacted to this warning by slamming the hypocrisy of those supposedly fighting for 'freedom', my friend had looked at me as if it had all been my own fault.

"Your head's cut, Mike – what's going on has got damn all to do with freedom. Republicans and Loyalists have the whole thing sown up between them. If I were you I'd take myself offside for a while."

I had always intended to travel, but circumstances had conspired to make an early departure seem more than prudent.

So now, when the Pakistani villagers walked by, proudly sporting their weapons like badges of manhood, I could only see the despair and the grief of the mounting toll of innocent victims in Ulster's senseless war.

• • •

"What part of Belfast are youse from then!"

The voice startled us, seemingly floating disembodied from a direction we could not immediately identify. In front of us all was quiet and deserted, save for a lone villager, his white wraparound dhoti gently swirling about his legs, leading a water buffalo through a field of sugar cane. Beyond him we could just make out the top of the buildings which enabled us to locate the town of Taxila. If anywhere should have seemed a world away from Belfast, it was here.

I turned around but there was no-one in sight, and we knew that shortly before, when we had strolled out onto the porch of Taxila Youth Hostel – the first official Youth Hostel we had used in Asia – it had been empty except for the two staff, and, according to the visitor's registration book, had been so for some time.

"I'm up here."

Straining our eyes against the sunlight we looked above us and, sure enough, a face peered down from an upstairs balcony. It suddenly withdrew and we waited, soon detecting the sound of footwear clipping against the stone floor. The face's owner finally emerged from the doorway and seated himself wearily beside us.

"Christ, but it's hot here."

He opened his shirt-front a little more and wafted the material a number of times.

"Well – what part? I'm from the Cregagh Road myself."

"Last address was a flat in Fitzroy Avenue. How did you know we were from Belfast? From the register?"

"Nah, I haven't signed in yet – just arrived. A couple of days ago some people, when they heard where I was from, told me a Belfast couple were travelling up ahead. When I saw you two I figured it was you."

The travellers' grapevine was like that. Not only was vital information about hassles ahead or good places to stay eagerly conveyed along it, but messages could be left for people following behind, with a fair chance they would reach their intended recipients. This was possible because many Asian countries, despite their vast size, possessed a relatively small number of major trunk routes, and you could invariably predict where travellers' itineraries would eventually intersect.

"So, what brought you both to Taxila? The Buddhist ruins?"

Exactly that, we confirmed. After returning from the Swat valley and rejoining the main road to Lahore, we had decided to divert here, because of the important archaeological ruins in the vicinity, dating from between 600 BC and 600 AD.

"What about you?"

"Well, for the last two years I've worked around England, spending two weeks' holiday getting stoned with mates in Bournemouth. Anyway, one of them told me that dope is real cheap in Goa and you can live there for the *whole summer* for less cost, so I thought I'd give it a try."

We looked at him in astonishment.

"You're travelling the whole way overland . . . just to smoke dope in Goa! No other reason? What made you stop at Taxila, then?"

"Well, you're right, it did seem a bit rash, so I thought I'd better justify my time and see a few things."

We all fell silent for a while and continued to contemplate the peaceful countryside, now completely devoid of people, a rare enough occurrence in many parts of Asia.

"Have you seen them yet?"

"Seen . . . ?"

"The ruins."

"Yes. Yesterday."

"And? Are they worth it?"

"They're interesting enough, though it's a bloody hot walk getting there."

That was an understatement, for the previous day we had zigzagged from one side of the road to the other, just to have the benefit of the shadows cast by any of the trees which lined it, even if each only provided a fleeting respite from the intensity of the sun.

"How far away are they?"

"The best ones are probably four miles . . ."

"Four miles! Christ, I'll not bother with that!"

Nor did he. Somehow the long journey overland to Goa and its cheap dope was acceptable, but four miles up a scorchingly hot road to Buddhist ruins was taking things just a bit too far.

• • •

Lahore was a real bustle of people, cows, water buffalo, taxis, trishaws and swirling dust. The hot, itchy, tiring eight-hour journey from Rawalpindi had allowed us to savour the friendliness of the Pakistani people, and now, walking through the bazaar area in Lahore, that friendliness asserted itself anew.

The hospitality shown by one of our hotel staff had not been entirely without ulterior motive, however, something we should have suspected when the young man welcomed us just a little too enthusiastically.

"Come in, come in! You are tired. Come and rest."

He hurriedly escorted us to our room and helped us unload our backpacks, then indicated for Sheila to recline on the bed. Instinctively wary, she nevertheless did as he bid.

"Are your shoulders in pain?"

Sheila glanced at me, unsure.

"I know what is very good for them."

He stood at the head of the bed, bent forward and placed his hands on Sheila's neck. At first she tensed, then made a conscious effort to relax.

"Is that good? I am an expert at this."

He continued to knead Sheila's neck muscles gently and she allowed her eyes to close. Then his hands gradually began to slip down inside the front of her blouse, and, realisation dawning, her hands flew up protectively.

"Thank you, that's enough!"

He backed away at her assertiveness and fumbled his way to the door.

"Okay, have a good rest. See you later."

When the door closed behind him, Sheila and I burst into laughter. I plonked myself down onto the other bed and glanced over at her.

"I should really continue where he left off, I suppose, but I'm just too tired."

I need not have worried, for Sheila was already fast asleep.

• • •

Because of the celebration feast marking the end of Ramadan the border with India was to be closed for three days, but we were content to linger, for there was an amazing vibrancy about Lahore. It was a chaotic vibrancy, bombarding us with a kaleidoscopic swirl of images: water buffalo dominating any areas of shade; garish movie billboards obliterating the entire façades of buildings; the hectic flurry of sellers and customers around the numerous street stalls; turbaned snake charmers demonstrating their talents outside the massive walls of Lahore Fort; the dizzying rush of trishaws conveying their passengers in and out of the traffic with unerring accuracy.

Our hotel manager invited us to his home for the celebratory feast and the evening was spent in relaxed conversation, mostly with his father, a retired army officer and lawyer who, interestingly, had spent some time in Belfast and Derry during the Second World War.

• • •

The next day we departed for the Indian border, only to receive a shock on our way there. A routine check of our money belt revealed that while our traveller's cheques and US dollars were undisturbed, 600 German marks were missing. The only time the money belt had been left unguarded was on the day of our arrival in Lahore when, after our initial doze, I had gone for a shower thinking Sheila had fully wakened, only to return and find that she had fallen asleep again in her exhaustion. She vaguely recalled hearing someone enter and move around the room but thought that it had been me. There was nothing we could do about it now, except learn from the experience.

At the border town of Wagah we watched in amusement the method of transferring goods from one country to the other. A long line of *red*-coated porters would bring boxes from a Pakistani lorry up to a white line chalked out on the ground, and there, supervised by officials, hand them over to another long snaking line of *blue*-coated Indian porters who would in turn deposit them on an Indian lorry.

India (i)

(27 September – 20 October 1976)

After visiting the magnificent Golden Temple in Amritsar – the holy city of the Sikhs – we boarded a train to Jammu, for we wanted to explore Kashmir before we made our way into the heat of central India. The train journey was marred by something I now feared was going to become a regular occurrence – once again I was sick and spent an inordinate amount of time locked in the toilet. On arrival in Jammu I felt so ill I realised that there was no way we could proceed to Shrinagar, and we managed to obtain 'floor space' at the Government Rest House for two rupees each. I lay all night with an extremely high fever, never having felt so helplessly weak before.

The following day the fever had only slightly abated and Sheila had fallen ill as well. The day passed in a blur, punctuated with friendly local people periodically administering – despite our feeble protests – a varied and frightening assortment of antibiotics. By evening we felt just about able to walk to the train station to buy curd, but our legs protested every step of the way.

The next day we were still weak but desperately wanted to escape our surroundings, and so we secured places on a bus to Shrinagar. It too, as we had anticipated, was an extremely tiring journey and we arrived in a debilitated, exhausted state, endeavouring to battle our way through the horde of hotel and houseboat touts awaiting us at the station. We finally agreed to take a room on one of the houseboats, simply because the youth touting for it was not so irritatingly pushy as the others. In semi-darkness he led us to the shore of Lake Dal, and even in our enervated state we revelled in the refreshing coolness of the air and welcome sight of the gently undulating waters of the lake, aglow with an evening luminescence.

As we stepped onto the houseboat, feeling the wooden deck resonate under our feet and hearing the gentle lapping of water against the main supports, we had the feeling that we would soon be on the mend.

・ ・ ・

Making our approach to the Thajiwas Glacier provided an opportunity to reflect upon the diversity of India. For many in the West their image of India is either one of hot desert landscapes dotted with poor villages and watched over by romantic castles and turbaned tribesmen, or of the chaotic downtown areas of Mumbai (Bombay) and Calcutta filled to bursting with bustling humanity. Yet India also has a strong foothold in the mighty Himalaya, with its share of places of solitude and remoteness.

We had taken a bus from Shrinagar to Sonamarg – 'Golden Meadows' – an ideal location from which to fully appreciate the grandeur of the Vale of Kashmir. There we deposited our backpacks in the chalet-style restaurant whose floor became a travellers' dormitory in the evenings. Our sleeping arrangements thus settled we were free to undertake the four-kilometre walk to the glacier at our leisure, enthralled by the bracing beauty of its magnificent setting.

・ ・ ・

As I surveyed the interior of our carriage I realised that this train journey possessed all the elements of a potential nightmare.

We were travelling 'third class unreserved' from Jammu to Delhi and the next thirteen hours were going to be an experience we would never forget, no matter how much we might try. Even before we left Jammu our carriage had been full, but now, with no-one getting out at any of the stations en route but more and more people squeezing in, to say that the carriage was becoming overcrowded would be quite an understatement.

Men, women and children occupied every conceivable inch of space: perched tightly together on the luggage racks, their legs dangling in the faces of those below; huddled together outside the toilets; or forming part of the dense patchwork quilt of human beings which carpeted the floor. We found ourselves among the ones crammed together like sardines on the floor, crushed and sat upon by our fellow passengers, and in turn crushing and sitting upon them. A trip to the toilet required a Tarzan-like ability to swing from luggage rack to luggage rack, or walk upon shoulders and limbs – for the actual floor of the carriage was quite inaccessible – only to find a sleeping body jammed against the toilet door and have to retrace all your steps to the toilet at the other end of the carriage and hope that it was both free and accessible.

At each station newcomers would battle for non-existent places, a few individuals trying to bunk the queue by squeezing through any of the windows which were missing some of their protective bars, their luggage bouncing off the heads of anyone unfortunate enough to be in the vicinity, and then they themselves slithering over the tightly-compacted mass of humanity already inside the carriage. These efforts were always doomed to inevitable failure and we wondered what on earth such optimism was based upon. Had they never undertaken this journey before, did they not know what to expect? At times we began to feel quite apprehensive, wondering how we would ever escape if too many people tried to get in and would not take "we're full" for an answer.

Sleep – for us, at least – was impossible, and when we tried to doze we did so leaning against other bodies – there was no way we could lie down – and the hours ticked way in a claustrophobic haze. We resolved never to travel long-distance again without a sleeper reservation, but that was for the future, and we still had to get this nightmare journey over with.

• • •

None of the Asian cities we had passed through on our journey eastwards had prepared us for Delhi. The city was a blur of movement; incessant, unstoppable movement – of buses, taxis, trishaws, ox-carts, cows, hand-carts and mopeds, not to mention human beings by the thousands. This movement enveloped us like a blanket, at times suffocating, at times reassuring, and into which was woven a startling array of sounds, a pungent host of all-pervasive aromas and a staccato-like sequence of rapidly changing images. Old Delhi in particular, with its teeming street life, was an experience without equal, a relentless and simultaneous assault upon all the senses.

We did all the touristy things: visited the Red Fort, the Jami Masjid, and Chandi Chowk. Then we sorted out the more practical things, like visiting the Nepalese embassy for visas and calling at the GPO to collect letters from home. We also required gamma-globulin injections for protection against hepatitis while in Nepal. This protection, however, soon wears off, so rather than getting the injections in Belfast we had hoped to obtain them in Delhi. But in reality it was not so straightforward, and when visits to two hospitals resulted in failure a doctor advised us to try a chemist. It seemed an odd suggestion, but that was where we finally obtained our inoculations, administered by the chemist behind a curtain at the rear of his shop.

• • •

We moved aside instinctively as the two trishaws – cycle-rickshaws – almost locked their wheels together. The nearest one swerved clear and its rider quickly resumed his pursuit.

"Okay – only three rupees each! I take you to cheap hotel."

"No, thanks, we walk. Our legs are stiff . . . after the train."

He neatly positioned his trishaw to cut off his oncoming rival.

"Okay – two rupees. Very cheap."

We almost succumbed, but proceeded on towards the main road outside the railway station in Agra. We normally preferred to walk, and anyway, the customary twenty yards or so had not been completed. After that distance the *true* price usually materialised, although this time we were in for a shock.

"Okay, I take you free. Very good hotel."

I stopped abruptly – I had no choice, as his trishaw cut right across our path – and stared pointedly at him.

"Free? But back there you started off at five rupees each?"

He smiled that suspiciously benign smile which always left me wondering what the catch was.

"No, no, sahib – free. I like to help the foreign peoples."

Sheila and I gaped, dumbfounded and disbelieving. His unexpected offer had caused us to hesitate – a fatal thing to do with taxi-drivers and rickshaw owners. Before we knew what was happening he had leapt from his saddle and Sheila's backpack was being taken from her half-heartedly protesting shoulders. He waved derisively at his rival, who had already begun to seek other custom. But I was still unconvinced and resisted his attempts to remove my own backpack.

"No-one takes 'foreign people' around for nothing. Come on – tell us the truth."

A wide grin creased his features and his eyes twinkled mischievously.

"Okay. I get commission from hotel. You come?"

I laughed and nodded, releasing the tension in my back to enable his eager hands to accomplish their task.

"We will also give you four rupees for taking us there – okay?"

His grin grew even wider, and making sure we were both on board – and a precarious 'on board' it was – he began to pedal away from the station, his efforts soon accompanied by such a mixture of panting and sweating that my feeling of guilt rose with each revolution of the wheels. Perhaps too many photographic images of lazy colonial sahibs and their sweating coolies were haunting my imagination, but it felt so wrong to be thus transported. To ward off my guilt I tried to keep in mind the admonition we had recently received from a somewhat irritated Delhi businessman: "So you would rather walk, and not let them make a living?" But the exertions they had to go through, the agony? "Do you not think they are accustomed to that?" But the image of white foreigners being so pampered? "Who has the real problem with that? Them – or you?"

And all the while our new acquaintance chatted amicably – if at times a little breathlessly – over his shoulder.

"You want to see Taj tomorrow? I take you to Taj, then to 'baby-Taj' – Itimad-ud-Daulah – then to Fort . . . for two rupees each."

"Four rupees only! Come on – the truth!"

His laughter reassured us of his genuineness.

"Okay. I also take you to some shops after. If you buy anything, they give me commission, and one rupee even if you do not. Okay?"

I laughed and nodded agreement as he turned to give us a quick glance.

"Okay, it's a deal. How many shops?"

"Ten?"

"Ten! Look, we'll see how it goes. But we don't buy anything – just look."

"Yes, yes. Only look."

I smiled to myself at his persistence, once again amazed that necessity had accomplished for these youths' foreign language skills what years of schooling had failed to do for ours.

• • •

Because so many superlatives had been used to describe the Taj Mahal we remained cautious that much of this praise might be pure hype, and prepared ourselves for a possible disappointment. Our caution, however, was proven to be entirely without foundation.

Our trishaws deposited us outside the massive gateway which allowed entrance to the walled complex within which the famed 'monument to love' sat. And although we had already gained tantalising glimpses of the Taj from different part of Agra, we were now overwhelmed by the image displayed before us. From where we stood beautiful gardens stretched with unimpeded view to the front of the gleaming white marble structure, its shape mirrored in the tranquil waters of a long watercourse which ran the length of the gardens. The Taj Mahal was truly the most magnificent building we had ever set eyes upon.

For the next hour as we repeatedly circumambulated the building, awed by its sheer magnificence, or stopped to inspect the extraordinarily fine relief carvings which adorned so much of its dazzling surface, we readily acknowledged the veracity of another of the characteristics attributed to the Taj Mahal – that no words could ever do justice to this amazing building.

• • •

"Come, we take you to shops now."

We resumed our places in the trishaws – our friend of yesterday having brought along a colleague.

"You can tell the shop-owners you wanted one rider each – it means we *both* get a rupee."

They soon halted at the first stop on their planned itinerary and a tall man beckoned us inside, straightway going to some lengths to assure us that this was not really a shop. The first portion of the building seemed to support his contention, for here were a dozen young boys, none looking older than fourteen years of age, engaged industriously at various tasks.

"All these boys are descendants of the craftsmen who built the Taj. All the marble work in Agra is done only through family connections – all Muslim, I might add. Here you see the boys going through their apprenticeship. That one, for example, is drawing the design on a piece of marble; that one is chiselling it out; and those others are shaping the pieces of coloured stone – although in this case, of course, you can see it is mother-of-pearl he is working with – to fit in the gouged-out pattern."

Our guide's English was as precise as the boys' workmanship. He called one of the youths over and showed us where the sides of his fingernails had been completely worn away as a result of constantly holding the minute pieces of material against the hand-operated grindstone.

"These small objects that they are making are, of course, to be sold. Let me take you into the next room to view some of their handiwork – not that we expect you to buy anything. We are mainly interested in showing visitors how our small factory operates. Come."

Sheila and I exchanged disbelieving glances and followed him into an adjoining showroom, where for a good five minutes we were lost in admiration at the amazing display of craftsmanship arrayed before us. Our guide held up a large, beautifully inlaid marble chessboard.

"The boys, of course, only make some of the smaller items. This has been made by a master craftsman."

We peered intently at the delicateness of the work, our captivated interest swamping our desire to explain our true position to him. But it had to come.

"This is all truly beautiful. But before you show us any more, we must explain that we are not able to buy anything. We will be travelling a long time and cannot carry any extra weight."

Completely ignoring this statement, he continued to display more objects, while we continued in our embarrassed hedging, and it became obvious that he was not going to take "no" for an answer. Almost three quarters of an hour after entering we finally managed to extricate ourselves, leaving the disgruntled shop-owner fuming behind us, his former nonchalance all but evaporated.

The next shops followed the same pattern and by the time we had wormed our way out of buying "precious stones for your wife" and various other items, our heads were literally throbbing from the sales-pressure. I looked squarely at our trishaw driver.

"I'm sorry, friend, I had no idea it would be like this. No more – our heads our spinning."

"But you said ten!"

"No, *you* said ten – I said we would see."

"Just one more. Only one."

I took a deep breath, torn between his pleading and the thought of the intense sales-pitch we would again be subjected to.

"Okay. But this is the last one."

This time it was another marble showroom and we had browsed for what we considered a reasonable enough time when we espied the assistant, having just 'wrapped up' some other customers, head in our direction. In our haste to make a quick exit, my day-pack, containing our camera, swung against a two-foot square replica of the Taj, neatly whipping off one of the corner minarets. Our hearts sank as we watched the object bounce onto the floor. We raised our eyes to meet those of the assistant, who bravely tried to hide his agonised expression, his voice croaking as he spoke.

"Never mind. Can be fixed. Can . . . can I interest you in some of our craftwork?"

And so we had to prolong our stay, mumbling utterances of appreciation at each new item and feeling so guilty. I was avoiding his eyes when at last I spoke.

"We will have to think it over. We will come back tomorrow."

Annoyed by our feeble lies, we rejoined the two trishaw riders, quickly handed them a few extra rupees and before they could react made our way off down the road, breathing in the fresh air as if we had just emerged from imprisonment.

•   •   •

Even though the couple had been captured in the act of sexual congress the look on the woman's face was serenity personified, while that of her

76

companion – despite his aroused state – was almost whimsical. No aggressive baring of the teeth here, no rampant lust on display – just an overwhelming sense of union. A union not only between man and woman, but between love and sex. And there were so many of these happily copulating couples: carving after carving, in tier upon tier, adorned the temple's outer facade. Some voluptuous nymphs stood alone – the apsaras – and stared down at the spectator with such seductive intent it was hard to accept that they were indeed made of stone. Somehow the sculptors had invested their creations with an essence which transcended the medium in which they had chosen to work.

These extraordinary temples of Khajuraho, upon discovery by the Victorian English, had been condemned as 'India's shame', but gazing up at such happy sexuality, it was clear where the real shame had lain. There was a deep sense of reassurance about the copulating couples, a confirmation that here at least were images of sex which revealed its naturalness, its exuberance and its sensuality, far removed from that so-called eroticism which was often only a mask for exploitation.

• • •

While it was pleasant to linger at so many places, at times the need to cover the vast distances ahead of us necessitated spurts of rapid movement, during which people met and places visited remain only as a blur. On such spurts tiredness militated against any proper diary-keeping, yet the brief notes which were entered serve as a reminder of the momentum:

Sun 17 Oct . . . departed Khajuraho on exhausting bus ride to Satna, then train to Allahabad. Slept in retirement room for 5 rupees each – very clean.

Mon 18 Oct. Train to Patna. Luckily this time we got seats easily. Crossed the Ganges by steamer. Stuck at Sonepur awaiting the 11.45pm train to Raxaul on Nepal border. It may not arrive early enough and we're debating whether to hold off a day so as not to miss any Nepal valley scenery.

Tue 19 Oct. Decided to take last night's train anyway. Very tiring journey to Raxaul. During the night railway guards brought us into a sleeper for a rest, but we were shifted again at 5am. Badly bitten on the legs (through our clothes) by mosquitos. Didn't arrive in Raxaul until late afternoon. Booked into 3-rupee hotel and plonked ourselves down under mosquito net (rarely provided). Had early night.

Wed 20 Oct. Up at 5am, but bus from Birganj, just across border in Nepal, didn't leave until 10.30am, so arrived in Kathmandu in the dark.

Nepal

(20 October – 16 November 1976)

When we arrived in Kathmandu its citizens were celebrating Tihar, the Festival of Lights. The first day of Tihar is dedicated to crows, the second to dogs, the third to cows. We had arrived too late to see in what manner the inhabitants manifested their adoration for crows, but the other two species were garlanded with necklaces of flowers, the cows having the additional privilege of being painted as well. Yet despite this splurge of colour the temples and streets in the old parts of the city were littered with rubble and covered with dirt. And although the strikingly good-looking Nepalese people looked very clean in their bright clothes, roads on the outskirts were littered with human excrement every few yards and in the early morning hours we observed children squatting by the roadside, making little attempt at concealment.

The hippies of the 1960s had obviously found the city amenable enough, and even now there was lingering evidence of their presence, though we were informed that many had decamped for the lakeside at Pokhara, our next destination. But wandering around the 'Freak Street' area we could see why Kathmandu would have held such an appeal. The populace, always pleasant and courteous, were not so pushy as elsewhere in Asia and visitors who just wanted to relax were allowed to do so. Also, the heavy concentration of exotic religious buildings around Durbar Square provided the perfect backdrop for those immersed in the spirituality of the East, while the almost bohemian look of the Freak Street area, with its clothes shops, esoteric bookshops, vegetarian restaurants and other haunts, readily created the necessary sense of alternative community within which a counter-culture could consolidate and flourish.

Out of some vague sense of solidarity we entered a self-styled hippie restaurant and made ourselves comfortable. The staff were not in any great hurry to serve us – presumably an obligatory part of hippie culture – and it was lucky they were not, for when we saw the prices on the menu card we made as laid-back but as hasty an exit as we could, retreating to a place where the locals ate and where we knew the fare was not only wholesome but inexpensive. We did, however, give in to an insistent sweet tooth and indulged in more than the occasional chocolate and banana cake, or chocolate and apple cake, in one of the famed pie-shops.

One notable stop on our sightseeing list was Swayambhunath, known as the 'monkey temple'. Perched atop a small hill and fronted by clanking prayer wheels, the main stupa was conspicuous for the large and brightly-painted 'seeing eyes' which stared down from all four sides of its upper plinth. In the courtyard within the temple complex young monkeys chased each other around like kittens, while teenage novice monks in their saffron robes sat chatting together on benches.

After three months of constant travelling, Kathmandu had come at an appropriate moment. The easy-going pace of our daily routine in the Nepalese capital, our unhurried walk to nearby Patan, our leisurely browsing among narrow side-streets searching out half-hidden temples, our visit to the National Theatre for a performance of music and dancing, even our sorties into the pie-shops – all this we knew was a very necessary recharging of our batteries.

· · ·

We were stunned when we looked out through our bedroom window. Low cloud had reduced visibility when we had arrived in Pokhara by bus from Kathmandu, and finding the town too grubby had made our way to Lake Phewa, seeking quieter accommodation and preferably a room with a view. And what a view we now beheld! There before us, in all their splendour, were the white summits of the Annapurna range – the various peaks which comprised the long ridge of Annapurna Himal itself and, most striking of all, Machhapuchhare, the Fish-Tail mountain. Breakfasting hurriedly, we carried chairs into the garden and for the next hour gazed in rapture at this superb sight. Travelling across deserts and plains it is easy to forget temporarily the lure of mountains, but once you are again in their presence the sheer magnetism returns with all its forcefulness. We were anxious to begin our trek.

We had decided not to contemplate the most renowned walk – the three-week trek to Everest. Firstly, we were not properly equipped for such a lengthy trek; secondly, we were concerned that our recurrent bouts of 'traveller's tummy' might have depleted our reserves of stamina. Instead, we decided on a trek to Annapurna Base Camp. Treks in the Annapurna region offered the best food and accommodation facilities for independent trekkers. Secondly, of all the treks in Nepal the one to Annapurna Base Camp took you high into the mountains in the shortest period of time, and, most importantly, the final destination – Annapurna Sanctuary, a natural amphitheatre surrounded by eleven peaks over 21,000 feet – allowed trekkers, as one guide book noted, entrance to a fabulous mountain realm normally the preserve of mountaineers.

But for the moment we had to contain ourselves; we had set aside a few days for simply relaxing, buying food supplies for the trek and gathering information on our proposed route. The first two of these tasks were the easiest to accomplish, the third frustratingly elusive. All along the shore of Phewa Lake there were numerous tourist lodges and restaurants, frequented by a sizeable hippie contingent. Going by our experience so far, we assumed that among this community would be a fair sprinkling of travellers and trekkers. Perhaps there were, but in those two days we never unearthed any. Time and again we would sit beside groups of young people and try to glean trekking information. One conversation with a young, blond-haired Western male at the start of our information-quest established the pattern for those to follow.

"Have you been into the mountains yet?"

"No."

"Not long here, then?"

"Been here quite a while."

"Do you not leave the lake."

"Sure, I bus it into Kathmandu when I need to renew my visa."

"No desire to go trekking, then?"

"Nah. The mountains *are* beautiful, mind you. But I'm 'high' enough here, man."

With that he smiled broadly, took another long drag of his joint and offered it to us. We declined and watched as his partner, an equally blond girl whose thin features were accentuated by the long muslin dress she wore, rolled another joint with well-practised ease.

We averted our eyes and gazed again at the stupendous view of those rugged peaks, still bewitched by the sheer beauty of Machhapuchhare – the whole panorama beckoning irresistibly. No, Sheila and I were definitely not high enough yet.

In the event, we began our trek with no information other than the rudimentary map we had purchased in Kathmandu. However, we had not proceeded far beyond Pokhara when we encountered a steady stream of trekkers making the return journey, and realised that information would be readily enough gathered along the trail. We should have guessed where all the trekkers were to be found – out trekking.

• • •

"Well, what else are you carrying in that rucksack, if you've only got two sleeping-bags and a tent with you?"

The Dutchman lifted our backpack by its shoulder straps and stared at us, perplexed. Feeling slightly embarrassed, I tried to appear as nonchalant as I could when I answered.

"Twenty hard-boiled eggs, twenty oranges, five loaves, one jar of honey, ten bananas, a bag of toffees and twenty-five small packets of biscuits – the biscuits are cheaper buying in quantity."

I paused to see how he would react to this inventory, but his eyes were on the backpack again, looking at it with new understanding.

"In the two days it took us to get here to Chumrung we were obviously able to buy food along the way. And we reckon that when we leave here – this being the last village – it'll take one day to get to Hinko Cave, another day to Annapurna Base Camp, perhaps a day there – depending on the weather – and two returning. That makes five days without food; so we'll consume a fifth of our supply daily."

The arrival of our smiling hostess carrying steaming plates of porridge ended the conversation and the six of us – we two on the ascent; the two Dutchmen undecided, as they had no sleeping-bags and were worried about the night temperatures at Base Camp; and a French couple on their way down, who only greeted our requests for information with evasive grunts – dug into the huge helpings with fervour.

Our stomachs filled, for the moment at least, we leant back against the wall of the wood and stone-built house which served as chai-shop, restaurant and lodgings, and gazed anew at the beautiful view of Annapurna South and Hiunchuli towering ahead of us. Somewhere up the valley to our right lay our route. My eyes wandered away from the white peaks to the green countryside, the steep slopes utilised to the maximum with contour-hugging terraces. Every available plot of arable land seemed to have been harnessed for crop-growing. Far below us some children skipped effortlessly up the same stone steps we had plodded along the previous evening, sweating and straining. And outside another lodge we could see a group of bare-footed porters loading up the large funnel-shaped bamboo baskets in which they carried food and camping equipment for the organised groups of trekkers. We wondered what special goods they were being asked to transport today, for we had already encountered porters carrying tables, chairs, cassette players and other such 'necessities'.

We rose, paid our hostess, patting our stomachs to convey our satisfaction, then shouldered our backpacks and resumed our ascent. 'Ascent and descent' would be a more accurate description of these trails, for every few miles all the height painstakingly gained ascending a ridge would seem to be completely lost when the trail inevitably descended, leaving you with the prospect of having to regain all that height surmounting the next ridge, only to see it lost again soon afterwards. Nevertheless, we *were* climbing inexorably higher into the mountains, from the almost three thousand foot elevation of Pokhara to our intended camp for the night – Hinko Cave – at just below ten thousand. And all the time we were absorbing the stupendous scenery and breathing in the refreshingly pure and exhilarating mountain air.

Descending travellers warned us that the terrain immediately ahead was much different from that which we had encountered on our approach march, and they were right. For the first time on the trek we did not have sprawling vistas on all sides, in fact ten to fifteen feet was our limit, as we climbed steeply upwards through hour after hour of tangled and obscuring bamboo forest. Then a chilling mist descended during the afternoon and the path dissolved into a muddy stream. And up and up it went, an exhausting climb which finally ended eight hours after it had begun when we arrived at the dismal, wind-blasted cut in the side of the valley wall known as Hinko Cave. That night our down-filled sleeping-bags felt like paper on top of us and only brief moments of shivering sleep were possible.

• • •

"What do you reckon? Think we've gone far enough?"

I could not believe I was really saying this, but the thought of another day like the one we had just endured was something I did not want to contemplate. The extremely strenuous climb had been a severe test of my stamina. I had hoped that a good sleep might have renewed our energy levels but sleep had eluded us and I just could not face further exhaustion. Was our indecision entirely due to the terrain, I wondered, or to our recurrent bouts of illness, which were so persistent we resolved to have a hospital check-up on our return to Kathmandu.

Sheila, just as tired as I was, had initially begun to enter into debate on what we should do, weighing up the pros and cons. Then her demeanour suddenly changed and she looked straight at me, speaking quietly but matter-of-factly.

"We've come this far; we're not turning back now."

I stared at her in astonishment. She was not inviting further discussion – as far as she was concerned, the matter was settled. I smiled and reached for my backpack.

"Okay, let's press on."

Sheila was right. It would have been a terrible mistake to have turned back. Not simply because the going was much easier than on the previous day and we reached our destination in just over four hours, but because of that destination itself. Annapurna Sanctuary was an incredible place. Our luck had held out in that there were no clouds to obscure our view – we had been informed that they usually came down by 10am – and we had two hours of unrestricted and spellbound viewing. For 360° we were surrounded by the magnificent peaks of the Annapurna range: Annapurna South, Fang, Annapurna I, Rocnoir, Gangapurna and Machhapuchhare.

When the clouds did eventually arrive to obscure our view they also brought a noticeable chill to the air and we decided that the Sanctuary had been as kind to us as it could and opted to begin our descent.

That evening lower down the valley we found a place near the trail to camp, and while the night was perceptibly warmer than the previous one we still awoke in the morning to find the tent covered in frost and quite stiff. When we were ready to set forth I had to carry it folded over like a huge sheet of cardboard, until it began to thaw out and we could pack it away.

And slowly we retraced our steps to Pokhara, our lingering memory of that frozen white skyline completely swamping any memories of the hardship encountered on the strenuous ascent.

• • •

"Michael and Sheila Hall!"

We arose and followed the nurse into a side room. A doctor was seated at a table, writing notes. He looked up and smiled.

"Yes, your stool-test results are back. You both have traces of bacteria."

"Is it serious, doctor? I mean – is it dysentery?"

He smiled again and put down his pen.

"Most of these things are a form of dysentery. Take these pills: three a day for five days."

He indicated for the nurse to escort us out.

"But will it clear up?"

He had already resumed his writing when he replied.

"Until the next time you get it."

As we walked away from the United Missions hospital outside Kathmandu, we realised that there was only one way to suppress our fretting – to treat ourselves to a chocolate and banana cake at a Freak Street pie-shop.

India (ii)

(16 November – 13 December 1976)

At the train station in the small Indian border town of Raxaul I presented our student concession forms – for onward travel to Varanasi – with just a slight hesitation. The young clerk smiled pleasantly and dutifully took them over to a side-office where we could see an older man sorting through papers. When he in turn was handed our forms he scrutinised them almost absent-mindedly and I began to feel that my concerns had been exaggerated after all. Then his eyebrows narrowed and he peered more intently at our forms. I knew it, I moaned, why did that woman in Delhi not believe me! The man – we presumed he was the stationmaster – rose to his feet with unseemly haste and strode purposefully to the counter. I smiled at him as disarmingly as I could, but when he spoke there was no hint of reciprocal pleasantness.

"You cannot have concession!"

His tone was so officious it immediately irritated me.

"Why not? What is the problem?"

He laid the form out before us and tapped a finger repeatedly on one particular line. I did not even have to look – I knew what line he was referring to. With a very noticeable hint of satisfaction in his voice he snapped:

"Look! Alteration!"

That woman, I fumed, that stubborn woman!

We had foreseen this problem arising as far back as Delhi. The hundreds of train stations all over India which served small towns and villages could only issue reduced-rate tickets on production of a concession form obtained in one of the larger towns. Alternatively, if travellers had a rough idea of their itinerary they could obtain any number of separate concession forms from one of the four major administrative centres within the railway network: Delhi, Bombay, Madras and Calcutta.

We had assumed that the concession office in Delhi would be close to the main railway station; it was not, and we had trudged for miles before we located it. By the time we got there it was almost closing time, a fact we were kept aware of by the woman who dealt with us, for she glanced frequently at a nearby wall clock. Nevertheless, she politely and efficiently – if a little hurriedly – recorded details of each of our proposed journeys, then issued the appropriate concession forms, along with multiple copies – something inevitable with paperwork in India. When she finally handed me the bundle of forms I knew she was expecting us to depart, but I glanced rapidly through them, giving each a quick inspection. She was just on the point of saying something when my eyes caught what I had feared: a mistake – on the concession which would take us from Raxaul on the Nepalese border to Varanasi.

I brought it to her attention and requested that a new form – with its attendant copies – be made out. With a hint of irritation she snatched the form back and hovered over it with her pen.

"Show me the mistake. I will amend it now!"

"Ah . . . just there. But we would prefer if you issued a new form . . ."

My protest was futile – she was already scoring out the mistake and writing the correct information above it.

"There is no need! Why would you want a new one!"

"Well, it might be thought that *we* made that change ourselves."

She seemed somewhat impatient now.

"Nonsense! A new form is not necessary."

"Okay, fine . . . ah, are you *sure* a new one is not possible?"

She glared at me with obvious annoyance.

"Do you not trust Indian people?"

Heavens, I thought, now she is playing the 'national honour' card! There was only one way I could reply.

"Of course I do. Thank you very much for giving us so much of your time."

As we walked away from her office, I felt a sense of guilt. Had I offended her, I wondered. Had my request been unreasonable? I hoped she would not put us down as just more demanding tourists. But, then again, we had seen Indian bureaucracy in action and were only too aware of the bureaucratic mentality. Indeed, some government offices, with their rarely-cleaned windows and their towering piles of dusty and discoloured paperwork, looked almost Dickensian. One friendly government official had said to us that "The British bequeathed us a bureaucratic legacy and we Indians duplicated it, then duplicated the duplication." Well, at least it served to provide jobs. As for the acceptability of our amended concession forms – only time would tell whose understanding of Indian officialdom was right and whose was wrong.

Mine had been right; hers had been wrong! As I now stood explaining the circumstances to our unyielding stationmaster, I suspected I was getting absolutely nowhere. He heard me out and then summarily dismissed my explanation.

"An alteration has been made to your forms and I cannot accept it. You will have to pay full fare!"

Although we were travelling 'on a shoestring', we could easily have paid the full fare, and while we obviously wanted our hard-earned savings to last as long as possible, we fully appreciated that foreigners' money made a necessary contribution to the local economy. But it had gone far beyond such idealistic considerations – the man's smugness had really irked me and I was now in as intransigent a mood as he. I tried again to remonstrate.

"Look, let me explain once more . . ."

"I am sorry, I have other things to do. If you want tickets, you must pay full fare."

And with that he gave me a last haughty stare, turned away with the hint of a smirk and beckoned his young assistant over to attend to us again.

That did it! Despite Sheila's insistent urging to drop the matter, I was fuming. What had started out as a minor problem had rigidified into a battle of wills. The young assistant came over to us, smiling pleasantly and looking a little disconcerted by it all. I smiled reassuringly, for the last thing I wanted was to redirect any of my annoyance onto the young man.

"You wish to buy tickets now?"

I stared at him for a moment then shifted my gaze to the older man who, despite having regained his desk – and despite supposedly having "other things to do" – was looking over at us with self-satisfaction writ large upon his features. He did not even avert his eyes at my gaze, but seemed more than content to stare me out. Think quickly, I said to myself, think quickly!

"Not yet, thanks. But I *would* like the Complaints Book."

The young man leaned closer; his older colleague noticeably stiffened.

"The . . . ?"

"The Complaints Book, please."

The young man looked taken aback, and the station master, for the first time, seemed caught off-balance. Under Mrs Gandhi's premiership an effort was being made to inculcate higher standards of behaviour in all aspects of public service, and as well as huge billboards exhorting citizens to practise family planning and "march towards a better tomorrow", every government office, every hotel, had its obligatory Complaints Book.

This time as I stared over at the stationmaster, there was a hint that he was ruffled. But it was only momentary, for he rose from his chair and approached us as nonchalantly as ever, and when he spoke to me he had lost none of his superior manner.

"And *why* do you require the Complaints Book?"

I returned his stare; I was beginning to warm to this.

"I wish to make a complaint."

He looked at me in surprise, and – or so I imagined – with some disdain.

"And what have you possibly got to complain about?"

I stared him squarely in the face.

"You."

He laughed haughtily.

"Indeed! Let me explain again to you. I believe that everything you have told me is the truth. But *you* were wrong not to insist upon a new form. The *office in Delhi* was wrong not to give you a new form. But *I* . . ."

He paused for added effect.

". . . *I* have done *nothing* wrong."

His features were now the perfect picture of smugness. So he was just keeping himself right – typical bureaucrat! He continued to stare at me dismissively.

"And if I have done nothing wrong, then there is nothing for you to complain about."

I returned his stare and paused for a moment before replying.

"I realise that if we had indeed falsified the forms then you *would* be making a mistake giving us tickets, and you choose not to take such a risk. That is what I wish to complain about – that we found you *more concerned about not making a mistake* than with trying to assist two foreign visitors."

The stationmaster's jaw dropped slightly and he looked as if he was about to speak, but no words issued forth. Obviously such an interpretation of our stand-off had not occurred to him. For some moments we stared at each other. My problem was that I was bluffing. A written complaint might, no matter how trivial, be held against the man, and I would never risk damaging anyone's security of employment. For all I knew, the stationmaster might have a large family to sustain. But would he call my bluff?

He turned abruptly and re-entered the side-office. A few moments later he summoned his assistant to his side. When the young man returned I looked to see if he was carrying 'the book', but he was empty-handed. He gave me the faintest hint of a smile.

"Your concessions are now accepted as good . . ."

I did not feel elated; in fact, I deeply regretted that it had all developed so ludicrously. I looked over at the stationmaster, nodded courteously, and without smiling – in case he misinterpreted it as a smirk – I mouthed the words "thank you". He gave an answering and equally courteous nod.

Four train changes later – during which we tried to snatch some sleep lying on a luggage rack – we arrived in Varanasi in the early hours of the following morning.

•　•　•

Our young boatman rowed us effortlessly along the murky waters of the River Ganges. The first rays of the morning sun were just catching the amazing assortment of buildings and temples which adorned the riverfront, tinting them with a warm ochre glow. The architecture of these buildings seemed without rhyme or reason, just a chaotic jumble of styles and shapes, which made it all the more fascinating. Some pyramid-shaped temples leaned at a precarious tilt, adding a strange dreamlike quality to the scene. A certain consistency was provided by the numerous *ghats*, the long flights of wide steps which led down to the Ganges. And on these *ghats* Hindus of all ages and classes were already beginning to assemble in small groups.

All along the riverfront with its pavilions and terraces sat numerous less-permanent structures – wooden platforms balanced improbably on tiers of large boulders. Here families would congregate together, or perhaps a holy man would hold court or sit in a meditative pose, under the shelter of a large bamboo umbrella covered with sackcloth or tightly-woven palm-fronds.

The great Hindu holy city of Varanasi, one of the oldest living cities in the world, has the Ganges as its throbbing heart. Other cities have grand squares, towering cathedrals or magnificent palaces as their core, the epicentre around which their citizens gravitate, but here all life – and death – radiated from the banks of this great river. As our boatman sculled silently from one *ghat* to another we could see that with each passing minute the tiny knots of individuals were becoming loose gatherings, some gatherings were becoming throngs and no doubt these throngs would soon become dense crowds.

Many people were already immersing themselves in the water, the men either stripped to the waist or girded only by a loincloth. The women ducked under the surface still wearing their saris and on re-emergence the brightly-coloured raiment clung tightly to their torsos. On regaining the lower steps of the *ghat* some women would loosen the folds of their saris and hold them away from their bodies, letting the warm air accelerate the drying process. People busily scrubbed their teeth in the water with index fingers or engaged in other forms of ritual cleansing. We leaned over the gunwale of the boat and peered into the brown opaque water, knowing that we could never contemplate following their example.

At one *ghat* we saw bodies being burned, the rising smoke signifying the final liberation of the soul from the endless cycle of death and rebirth. The behaviour of those gathered around the deceased made cremation seem quite an informal, almost irreverent affair, an image reinforced by the sight of a few holy cows wandering about among the ashes. Nearby, men were preparing piles of wood to meet the requirements of that day's customers.

Inevitably, alongside people's spiritual needs sat their material needs, and as we walked later through narrow streets we were constantly hassled by children, youths and adults all wanting to take us to "see silk shops". Our experience in Agra had taught us a lesson, however, and this energetic propositioning was singularly unsuccessful. At first we said a polite "no" to each request, but the pestering became so distracting we decided to ignore many of the more pushy touts.

That evening the family who owned our lodgings – an extremely large and good-looking family – invited us to a meal to celebrate the ten days which had passed since their mother's death. The eldest son – who, like most of the other males in the family, had shaved his head – told us that during this period of transition his mother's soul could be "troubled and wrathful", and as he in particular was in "most danger", he carried a knife and a ring for protection. The meal comprised an extremely varied selection of foods, all eaten with the fingers of the right hand from a leaf plate. The females of the family really took to Sheila, a situation we had already encountered elsewhere in Asia. Perhaps it was her quiet but warm personality, or the sincerity with which she responded to friendship, perhaps even her dark hair – for this was regularly commented upon – or more likely a combination of all these. At one stage they thanked her for showing "proper behaviour" during the preparation of the meal, unlike another of their guests, a Western female who had horrified their Hindu sensibilities – not to mention our more secular ones – by sticking her finger into the cooking pot to taste the food. After the meal the other visitors were permitted to leave, but Sheila and I were called to one side and asked to stay the rest of the evening.

• • •

Travelling long-distance on an Indian train is like sitting at the edge of a small town. All human life passes before you and if you are lucky you are occasionally invited to participate. The journey from Varanasi southwest to Jalgaon took twenty-five hours, but having booked a sleeper for the night part of it we felt much more relaxed than on other, shorter journeys. However, it was a rewarding experience largely because of the people we met, whether individuals, couples or whole families. Some were reticent at first to even make eye contact, but most people soon found some way – as did we – of initiating dialogue. With many, unfortunately, our conversations remained basic, but others had an excellent grasp of English and were often eager to engage in philosophical, historical or political debate.

Some castigated the British for their colonial past, but others defended that legacy with an enthusiasm which surprised us. One old man, a retired railway official, was quite outspoken in his opinions.

"Some people in India blame the British for everything – as I am sure they do in Ireland – but it was not all bad."

As he was obviously looking forward to having a good argument, I felt I should oblige.

"But do you not believe the British exploited India, its people and its resources?"

"Of course! But do you not think there were many Indians only too happy to exploit us, or many Irish only too happy to exploit the Irish? Most exploiters do not come from abroad – they live among us. In trying to control us the British destroyed the power of many rulers who had been exploiting the poor of India for a long time. Perhaps that was necessary. Perhaps the colonial experience helped us define what we wanted to be as a nation."

Not every conversation went so deep and most people were more concerned with finding out about our families, how many brothers and sisters we had, how long we had been married, how many children we would have, why I did not wear a wedding ring . . .

If children were present a rapport with our fellow-passengers was effected much sooner. Children, being no respecters of decorum or etiquette – certainly not on tedious train journeys – were not reticent in their behaviour, and once parents saw that we were responding positively they too would relax and smiles would be exchanged, to be soon followed by friendly conversation. We learnt as much about India – and its people's hopes and fears – from travelling along its railway network as we did from anything else.

When we disembarked at Jalgaon, we went by bus to the amazing rock-cut temples of Ajanta and Ellora, with a visit also to massive Khuldabad Fort, where, in centuries past, elephants had been used to batter down the massive entrance doors. However, because the doors were covered in spikes and elephants were precious commodities, more readily available camels had been used as buffers, their agonised death screams mingling with the frenzied trumpeting of the charging, drug-crazed elephants.

We then resumed our southwesterly train journey, and at our destination – Bombay – we discovered that India held yet more surprises for us.

• • •

Our first impressions of Bombay were somewhat disconcerting. Red double-decker London-style buses, grand and extravagant colonial buildings, modern office blocks – if it had not been for the teeming city life pressing in on us from every direction, and the cacophony of sounds which accompanied it, we might have wondered whether we were still in India. Somehow Bombay stood out as different. Perhaps it was because here Westernisation seemed to have progressed the furthest.

The social divide was more visible too, with images of the impoverished masses in the poorer districts juxtaposed with the sight of well-groomed, sharply-dressed businessmen striding purposefully about the cosmopolitan commercial centre. And where the two images collided – as when we saw a young boy crouched on the pavement outside one of the more affluent hotels, feeding on the lumps from someone's vomit – the contrast was all the more startling, the circumstances of the have-nots all the more offensive.

A few days after our arrival our social consciences received a further battering when, on a day-trip to nearby Juhu Beach, we passed an incredibly crowded and smelly shanty town composed of rickety wooden shelters and corrugated-iron huts, inhabited by the heaviest concentration of India's poor we had yet encountered. The fact that this city-outside-a-city existed so close to plush hotels and gleaming office blocks made me wonder yet again at the forbearance – or the inaction – of the world's destitute.

Staying at our hotel – which, although a budget one, was three times more expensive than anything we had encountered elsewhere in India – revealed another facet of Bombay life. During our first night, when venturing forth from our room to visit the toilet, I received quite a shock. The corridors and stairways were bunged solid with sleeping people, who had obviously come in off the streets during the night with the consent of the hotel owners. As I gingerly made my way between and around the limp figures I realised with a start that large rats were engaged at the same endeavour, hunting for scraps of food which might be secreted in folds of clothing or in the pitiful bundles of personal possessions. The creatures showed no fear at my approach and I had to place each foot down slowly and carefully in an effort to encourage any rat in the vicinity to move aside.

Then, a few minutes after I had returned to my single bed, I became vaguely aware that something was tickling my nose. I opened my eyes and leapt from the bed in horror, simultaneously sending the source of the tickling – a large cockroach – to the far side of the room with an involuntary sweep of my hand. In haste I searched around the framework of the bed, then between the slats supporting the mattress and discovered a whole colony of them. It took the violent deaths of fifteen of these creatures and the flight of their companions before I could bring myself to lie down again. Sheila had been woken by my exertions, but declined my offer to investigate her own bed, before quickly falling back to sleep again.

In the morning the corridors and the stairs were empty, save for a solitary member of staff busily sweeping. It was as if what I had seen the night before had all been in my imagination.

· · ·

Although on our first day we had been dismayed to find that money we had arranged to be sent to a bank in Bombay from Amsterdam had not arrived, forcing us to remain until our hurried telex would bring the desired response, we quickly grew to enjoy the city. In particular it felt good to be back beside the sea, and early evening strolls along Marine Drive were rewarded with glorious sunsets. A relaxing boat trip to Elephanta Island and its unique temple complex satisfied any obligation to engage in cultural explorations while the rest of the time we were content to wander the food stalls or mingle with the crowds on Chowpatty Beach.

One encounter, however, stood out above all the others. Towards the end of our stay we had to vacate our hotel because of a prior booking and decided to try and find one near Juhu Beach. It was a fruitless endeavour, but while engaged in it we were befriended by a taxi-man who insisted upon driving us around – free of charge – for two whole hours and aiding us in our search. Despite our repeated efforts to make him accept payment he adamantly refused, and when it finally became obvious that there were just no rooms available he further insisted upon paying our train fare back to the city centre. We just hoped that the enjoyable and light-hearted time we had spent together was some recompense for his unexpected generosity.

Another, much smaller inhabitant of Bombay filled me with guilt about the slaughter I unleashed each night upon our resident cockroaches. One afternoon Sheila and I were relaxing on our beds, reading, when our attention was caught by a noise coming from the small table positioned between us. There, totally unconcerned by our presence, sat a tiny mouse, contentedly nibbling at a remnant of bread. It was within an arm's reach of both of us, but although we sat up to observe it more closely, it just paused, sniffed the air, appeared to inspect both of us in turn and then resumed its eating. After some minutes watching in fascination we too resumed our reading, and over the next few days the mouse was to become a frequent visitor to the room. If I could 'live and let live' with this mouse, I asked myself, why could I not do the same with those cockroaches?

A week after wiring Amsterdam our money finally arrived and we purchased train tickets to Goa.

• • •

We had worked in Amsterdam for over a year before setting out on our Asian journey, leaving most of our earnings in a bank there, to be sent for when required.

We had been lucky to find work, for Amsterdam then was a thriving Mecca for young people from all over Europe and any job vacancies were greedily snapped up. When we had arrived the youth scene was so all-pervasive the city authorities had permitted a youth committee to establish 'sleep-ins' – cheap, hostel-type accommodation – and run a comprehensive youth support network. By day the city's multinational youth population congregated around the National Monument in Dam Square, watching and being watched, while at night they got high in music clubs like the Paradiso where soft drugs were openly available.

Amsterdam's central park – the Vondelpark – had also been appropriated. By day it was filled to capacity with young people, either lounging in small groups or gathered in circles around any budding musicians. Crowds were liveliest around those music-makers who beat out a driving rhythm on drums and tom-toms, usually to the accompaniment of hypnotic chanting from enthusiastic spectators. By night the park became one vast dormitory, with sleeping-bags and plastic sheeting indicating the whereabouts of those, like ourselves, who had been unable to find room in the sleep-ins, or who just wanted to sleep rough for the experience. A main road arched over a section of the park in the form of a mini-flyover, and in the walkway underneath an area had been sealed off for use as a depository for backpacks.

We had spent three weeks trudging the docks, the markets, the industrial estates, in a vain search for work. We made daily checks with the staff at various work bureaux, hoping that familiarity might result in job offers. Then, just as our finances began to run so low that we contemplated moving to Germany, we both struck lucky, with a temporary job in a pickle-bottling plant for me and a position for Sheila in the foreign section of a major bank. To any early morning park strollers it must have seemed quite incongruous to hear an alarm clock go off amid the sleeping bodies sprawled upon the grass, then watch as two figures hurriedly arose, rolled up their sleeping-bags and rushed off to the nearest exit. It was a difficult routine which luckily only lasted a short time, for one of Sheila's work colleagues lent us her apartment while she went on holiday and then other Dutch friends found us a vacant houseboat to rent.

The Dutch thought these were all terrible hassles to have to contend with, but to us they were not hassles at all. The Belfast we had left behind was a place of nightmares. As if the brutality of the IRA's 'armed struggle' was not enough, Protestant gunmen had been subjecting the citizens to a barbaric campaign of random assassinations, mainly directed at innocent Catholics but engulfing anyone who just happened to be in the wrong place at the wrong time. There were long periods when there was a new victim almost every night, and rumours of torture and mutilation had many people in a barely-contained state of panic. If you were unfortunate enough to have to move around the city after dark, even to go to your local corner shop, you held your breath when you heard a car approaching – particularly if you and the car were the sole occupants of the street – listening for the slightest indication that the vehicle might be slowing down, and when it was well past you released your breath in one long, tension-filled sigh.

Caught between the IRA's ruthless bombing and murder campaign and the Loyalist assassinations many communities were driven close to hysteria by the grinding, relentless terror of it all. As the body-count rose into the hundreds you realised that the police were quite impotent, and the stark reality was that here, in a Western European city in the 20th Century, you had as good a chance of meeting a brutal death as if you had been a mediaeval villager facing the turmoil of the Dark Ages.

It was indeed Northern Ireland's own return to the Dark Ages, and the tensions and stresses it engendered became lodged into your very being, became an almost invisible resident within your personality. We never realised just how insidious the whole process had been until, three months after arriving in Amsterdam, a comment from one of Sheila's work colleagues said it all:

"We were all talking about you the other day, and we agreed that when you first came you looked somewhat tense, wary. But that has slowly gone and you look far more relaxed now."

It was only then that we understood just how deeply it had affected us. Our relief at being out of that situation, however, was counterbalanced by our fears for those left to endure it, especially our families. Our only consolation was that they had been glad to see us go – our mixed relationship, not to mention my cross-community activities, would have provided sufficient reason for the bigots to have added us to their list of targets.

And gradually we reclaimed the freedom which had been stolen from us. Sometimes, in the early hours of the morning, we would leave our houseboat to go window-shopping in the deserted Kalverstraat, Amsterdam's pedestrians-only shopping street. Our Dutch friends had been horrified to learn of this, for to them the Kalverstraat at that time of the day was considered dangerous, the haunt of criminals and drug addicts. But to us it only mattered that it was not Belfast, and that was enough.

• • •

If it had taken us some time to unwind in Amsterdam, relaxation in Goa was instantaneous. There can be few places so idyllic and laid-back. Goa was a full day's train journey south from Bombay and during part of that journey we had the company of a Danish couple who holidayed in India for six weeks each year with their young children. We also had to contend with the largest concentration of beggars we had yet encountered. They would stand beside our seats, a hand held out expectantly, and just stare at us for ages. Perhaps they felt that by doing so we would eventually weaken, and if there had been only a few we would certainly have given each of them something, but their sheer numbers proved self-defeating. We may have been perceived as affluent by them, but our budget was tight and could never stretch to so many.

But at Colva Beach, Goa, gone was the incessant traffic din of Bombay, gone were the hands held out in supplication, gone – for the moment – was our guilt, and gone was our desire to do anything other than soak up the atmosphere of this exotic place and immerse ourselves in the beckoning surf. There were quite a few travellers and hippies about but not as many as we had feared, certainly not at Colva. Indeed Colva, to our delight, did not possess a single hotel. Instead, local people hired out rooms to travellers and we were soon settled in with a relaxed, gregarious family. Our room was bare of furniture apart from two beds, but it was cool and that was an important bonus. To wash we collected water from a communal well; the one we used served four households.

• • •

"OM MANI PADME HUM."

As we lazily dragged our feet through the surf we looked up the beach to see who was responsible for the chanting. There, as golden-skinned as the sand, sat four naked Westerners, two males and two females. But what was so striking about them was not their nudity, or that three of them were sitting cross-legged in the full-lotus position, but that they all had their eyes tightly closed. Certainly when meditating at home I too had closed my eyes, but then I had little to look at but four familiar walls, whereas here there was mile after mile of beautiful sand, fringed with gently swaying coconut trees, while further along the beach we could see a small group of fishermen straining every muscle to haul ashore one of their heavy outrigger fishing boats. If the object of meditation was to transcend the ego and become one with your surroundings, I was finding it much easier to attain such a state by keeping my eyes open.

The most laid-back and natural people about were undoubtedly the locals. The hardy, muscled fishermen and their ever-smiling womenfolk were so friendly compared to both the often aloof Westerners and the middle-class Indian tourists who arrived to gawk at the naked white buttocks and breasts.

The Goans possessed a quite distinct identity, partly the result of four hundred years of Portuguese influence and the unique blending of Hinduism and Christianity. But most notably they had little of that initial Indian reticence towards strangers and were readily communicative. I tried to assist some of the short, stocky fishermen drag one of their boats in from the tide and was astounded by the weight of it. Any strength rapidly deserted me and I looked at the fishermen in embarrassment, but they only responded with laughter and smiles.

We did not do all that much at Goa. We made one excursion into Panaji to check the Poste Restante and visit the Basilica of Bom Jesus with its remains of Francis Xavier contained in a silver casket. We did not, however, indulge in any further cultural or historical explorations, nor did we attempt to search out the main hippie scene at the beaches further north. We simply relaxed on our beach and sought out conversation with the dark-skinned Goans or the elderly Portuguese inhabitants.

But soon we knew it was time to move on and we took the train to Bangalore, then to Tiruchirapalli, where we booked a flight the following day for Jaffna in Sri Lanka. Our relaxing sojourn in Goa had refreshed us to the extent that while at 'Trichy' we resumed our cultural explorations with a visit to the remarkable temple complex of Srirangam.

Sri Lanka

(14 December 1976 – 11 January 1977)

As our plane had landed just before midnight we slept in the airport terminal, in the company of four other backpackers. With the dawn we bused into Jaffna – the main town in the northern, Tamil-inhabited part of Sri Lanka – but after spending a fruitless couple of hours searching for a budget hotel the six of us decided to take the train to Anuradhapura, one of the island's foremost historical sites.

On arrival at our destination we were approached by a hotel rep obviously on the lookout for young backpackers, but this tout was like none we had encountered before. Far from being pushy he was quite laid-back and we soon succumbed to his easy style and informative conversation. For a moment I thought that he was just someone astute enough to know what type of approach irritated backpackers, and had managed to develop a more appealing sales-pitch, but this suspicion quickly receded as he told us more about the organisation he represented.

He worked for one John B Paiva, who ran a budget hostel – Anuradhapura Travellers Halt, to which we were now being transported free of charge – and had linked a string of similar budget accommodations into an island-wide network. To help advertise this network Paiva published a free booklet, *Travel for the Young at Heart*, which was crammed with information about places to visit, entrance costs, possible excursions, advice on how to avoid theft on the trains, as well as a description of the facilities available at each of the hostels and family homes included in the network – most of which carried the name Travellers Halt.

There were also incentives for those who used only this network. Travellers coming to the end of their stay in Sri Lanka, for example, were offered free transport from Anuradhapura to Talaimannar Pier – where the ferry departed for India – provided they could produce receipts showing they had stayed in at least four of the listed hostels. It seemed, however, that his organisation had its competitors, for throughout the booklet there were numerous warnings: "Be sure you check in at Travellers Halt and not be misled in the vicinity!" "Beware of touts and bogus guides who will offer you cheaper places to stay with special bargains. You may, in the end, be paying more than what you expected of this bargain."

Among the incentives listed for staying at his own hostel in Anuradhapura was that "you could expect to meet many 'freaks' at the Travellers Halt where you could exchange notes of travel with fellow travellers." But of all the items in the booklet perhaps the most fascinating was a list of 'Travellers Ten Commandments'.

Thou shall not expect to find things as thou has them at home, for thou hast left thy home to find things different.

Thou shalt not take anything too seriously – for a carefree mind is the beginning of a vacation.

Thou shalt not let the other tourist get on the nerves – for thou art paying out good money to have good time.

Remember thy passport so that thou knowest where it is at all times – for a man without a passport is a man without a country.

Blessed is the man who can make change in any language – for lo, he shall not be cheated.

Blessed is the man who can say thank you in any language – and it shall be worth more to him than many tips.

Thou shall not worry. He that worrieth hath no pleasure – and few things are ever fatal.

Thou shalt when in Rome do somewhat as the Romans do; if in difficulty thou shalt use thy common sense and friendliness.

Thou shall not judge the people of a country by one person with whom thou has had trouble.

Remember thou art a guest in every land – and he that treateth his host with respect shall be treated as an honoured guest.

We were certainly looking forward to meeting this John B Paiva. Was he a bit of a 'freak' himself? Or was he just a typical businessman, only one with a shrewd eye for the backpackers' market? In fact he was neither, and we found him to be an easy-going, friendly individual who clearly enjoyed the company of the young travellers he catered for and seemed to have a genuine desire to be as helpful to them as he could. The pushy marketing which was so prominent in the booklet was absent from the relationships he formed so readily with his young guests. Some of the backpackers clearly appreciated the advice and support he offered, a reminder to us that for many young people the reality of long-haul travelling – with its often bewildering avalanche of new people, unfamiliar locations and unforeseen hassles – could get somewhat overwhelming and there were times when they needed to slow down and take stock.

• • •

Anuradhapura was founded as the capital of Sri Lanka in the 4th Century BC and remained so until the 10th Century AD. The ruins which survive contain many notable monuments highly sacred to Buddhists. However, the most revered site in Anuradhapura is occupied not by a man-made edifice but by a living tree, the Sri Maha Bodhi. The oldest historically authenticated tree in the world – over 2,200 years old – it is reputed to have been grown from a sapling from the very *bo* tree at Bodh Gaya in northern India beneath which the Buddha had gained enlightenment. This sacred tree has been continually attended, by hereditary guardians, for its entire existence, even when Anuradhapura ceased to be the capital of Sri Lanka and its monuments fell into disrepair.

We spent a relaxing two days wandering among the ruins, our explorations enhanced by the friendly reception we received from local people, especially the children who were forever smiling and offering flowers. When you added to that a rich profusion of birds, butterflies, monkeys and fruit bats the place exuded a magic all of its own.

When we departed Anuradhapura it was to visit another ancient capital. After Anuradhapura had been overthrown by South Indian invaders, the newcomers chose as their seat of power a site some sixty miles to the southeast – Polonnaruwa – and when this was eventually retaken by the Sinhalese the latter retained it as their new capital and began to construct a city to rival Anuradhapura, fortified with three concentric walls, beautified with parks and gardens and sanctified with numerous shrines. Some of the remains were quite spectacular, particularly a group of stone statues of the Buddha collectively known as Gal Vihara, one of the statues depicting a reclining Buddha 44 feet long.

But just when we had decided that Anuradhapura and Polonnaruwa would be hard to better, our next stop – the fortress of Sigiriya – did just that. Like the Jewish citadel of Masada, the fortress of Sigiriya is sited atop a huge rock which dominates the surrounding countryside. The final part of the ascent to the summit is guarded by two massive lion's paws carved out of the rock, all that remains of a gigantic lion through whose jaws visitors once had to pass. Beyond the paws present-day visitors still face a certain amount of trepidation because of the exposed and quite steep stairwell they have to traverse, assisted only by a handrail. On one portion of the rock is the most renowned of the fortress's attractions, the Sigiriya Maidens – brilliantly coloured wall paintings of voluptuous, bare-breasted females.

• • •

The booklet's warning had been correct! When we disembarked from the bus at Kandy not only were there two rival hotel reps waiting for us, promoting hostels with near-identical names, but Paiva's competitors had produced their own near-identical booklet. Or was *he* competing with *them*?

Kandy is the capital of Sri Lanka's 'hill country', a welcomingly cool location 1600 feet above sea level. It is famous for the Dalada Maligawa, the temple in which is enshrined Sri Lanka's most treasured possession – the Sacred Tooth Relic of the Buddha, brought to the island in the 4th Century AD. But before we visited the temple, the Botanical Gardens or the Elephant Bathing Place – the major tourist attractions – we were anxious to get our own teeth into some of the exotic food on display at the market. Backpackers must always get their priorities right.

At Nuwara Eliya, south of Kandy, we watched women at work picking the hill country's most famous produce, tea. We fell into friendly conversation with one of the tea-pickers, a Tamil girl who told us how unhappy her parents were that she had fallen in love with a boy from Sri Lanka's majority Sinhalese community. Shades of Northern Ireland, I reflected. However, our stay in the hill country was cut short by another common feature of the area – dense mist and torrential rain. We were disappointed, for we had intended to climb Sri Lanka's highest mountain, Mount Pidurutalagala, but when the rain proved unrelenting for two days, we decided that if Sri Lanka was anything like Ireland then there was little point in waiting around. If we were going to get this wet, we figured, it might as well be by sea water as by rain, and so we made our departure for the southern coast.

· · ·

We had now visited most of the Asian destinations considered to comprise the select list of 'in' places frequented by hippies and backpackers – Kabul's Chicken Street, Kathmandu's Freak Street, Pokhara's Lake Phewa and most recently Goa – partly because the roads led us there, partly out of curiosity. But we decided to give one other 'in' destination a wide berth – Hikkadua on Sri Lanka's southwest coast. Backpackers we met in Kandy told us that it was not only full of a noisy Aussie surfing contingent but that hepatitis was rife among some of the long-stay hippie residents. Instead, we decided to make for Matara. Why there? Well, the nearby Polhena beach was described in *Travel for the Young at Heart* as follows:

> The Matara–Polhena beach is noted for its stillness and sunny beaches where one could walk for miles into the sea, and the waves are ever friendly inviting you to walk even further with hardly any indication of being dashed on the water. Polhena beach is famous for sea bathing, with its enchanting bays, shoals of coloured fish and encircled with shining Coral Reefs.

How could we possibly resist?

The description was misleading in one of its claims, however, not that it troubled us much. If the beach was indeed famous it was a fame kept relatively secret, for in the eleven idyllic days we stayed there we encountered only four other Westerners.

It was here too that I introduced Sheila to snorkelling and the magical realm to which it provided entrance. Polhena Beach was an ideal location for a beginner, as there was no need to cover great distances in search of spectacular underwater life. Without extending our explorations beyond a dozen yards from the shore we would encounter an amazing variety of fish, flashing before us with an astounding diversity of colour. A coral reef a short distance further out to sea blunted the power of the breakers and the only drawback was that we became so engrossed our exposed backs got quite sunburnt. Those who have entered the underwater realm know that swimming on the surface can never be the same again.

• • •

As we lay on the hot sand after one breathtaking exploration, I recalled my first ever snorkel, in the cold waters of the Irish Sea, and the danger I had unwittingly exposed myself to. As I had walked back to our rented cottage in the small hamlet of Rossglass, my mask and snorkel dangling from my hand – one of the old-fashioned snorkels with a ping-pong ball encased in a small cage stuck on top, supposedly to prevent any water entering the tube while you were submerged – the owner of our cottage had called to me from the grocery shop he also managed. When I entered, dripping water onto his shop floor, he indicated to a stranger who was standing beside him.

"Wait till you hear what this man has to say to you."

His tone was so serious my immediate concern was that I had done something wrong, though I could not imagine what. For his part the stranger looked extremely grave.

"You're a very lucky boy, sonny. I was driving down the road there and I thought I'd take a few shots at the ducks. I saw this likely target – curved back, long neck, small head – so I rolled down my car window and took aim."

He paused and my heart raced, for I knew what he was going to say next.

"And then you stood up, son. Christ, you didn't half give me a fright! It was the top of *your head* and that contraption you're carrying there that I was looking at – I could've near blew it off!"

When I got home I did not tell my mother – there are certain things you just do not tell your parents.

• • •

"Do you think all this talk of a General Strike is true?"

I directed my question to the oldest and most respected member of the family in whose house we were staying. A wave of strikes was spreading across Sri Lanka; following a strike by railwaymen, other workers were coming out and there had been rumours of sabotage in the docks. The government was threatening to use the army to maintain essential services – indeed, soldiers were already unloading cargo ships. The old man looked around the gathering soberly, as if to lend dramatic weight to his serious mood, and shrugged his shoulders, before answering in the distinctive accent of the Ceylonese English-speaker.

"Who knows? Perhaps we are facing another '71. You know of '71? When this government suppressed a rural youth uprising leaving thousands dead?"

"Another uprising? Would the people support them again?"

The old man's hand smacked down hard on his knee, crushing to a bloody pulp one of the swarm of black and red-stripped mosquitos which inhabited the swamps around Matara. Whose blood was it this time, I wondered.

"I doubt it. However, '71 came so near to success that it showed people how powerful they could be. So it is hard to predict what might happen; things might turn very bad. As a bus strike has been called for the 6th, you two might be stranded down here if you do not get to the boat before that."

I nodded agreement. We had already reached the same conclusion and had informed the family that we would be departing in the morning. It was sad to have to leave, for the last twelve days had been idyllic: not just the two hours a day spent snorkelling, but our lazy wanderings along shady lanes, repeatedly answering the three questions local children had all learnt by heart: "What is your name? Where are you from? Where are you going?"

A movement outside the open window startled me. I peered into the darkness beyond to see the family's eldest son signalling to me. What on earth was he up to? As unobtrusively as I could I slipped away from the gathering and made my way towards the dark shape silhouetted by the moonlight.

"You want to see a turtle?"

"Love to. Where is it?"

"My friends find it on the beach. They hide it in the hut over there. They are going to kill it and then cut it up and sell it."

I shuddered in advance at the poor creature's fate.

"On second thoughts, I don't think I want to."

"Me too. I do not like to see all the blood. But do not tell anyone. You know we are not allowed to kill – as we are Buddhists."

"But will *you* eat it?"

"Oh yes. If I kill it, then I am in real trouble when I die. But if another person kills it, it is okay."

I could not help smiling at this rationalisation.

"Is that good Buddhism?"

"Well, my friends and I, we are . . . not so good Buddhists. Many people here still believe in magic. The Catholic priest sells magic 'snake-stones' that you rub on a bite to cure it. And my wife says her sore leg came because she caught a spell meant for someone else. She will not go to doctor."

He sighed and leaned against the rickety gatepost.

"Anyways, I am glad. It will get better soon; doctors are too much money for poor people."

• • •

The next day we stood waiting at the ramshackle bus depot for the bus which would take us to the capital, Colombo, finishing off a large pot of curd to the amusement of a smiling, joking crowd. And when the bus arrived, despite all our practice we were yet again beaten to the entrance by the jostling crush and I was forced to stand for the next five hours, with my head bent to one side as usual – rarely in Asia did I find a bus interior which could accommodate my height.

Not that it mattered, for soon after coming upon the first stretch of sharply curving roads most seats were urgently commandeered by females, who took turns at vomiting out through the open windows – women and children being notoriously bad travellers in Sri Lanka, a situation prevailing in other parts of Asia.

One seat, however, was not commandeered by a woman. It *had* been, but she had been forced to vacate it. This seat, a front seat which had a sign above proclaiming, in both Sinhalese and English, that it was "reserved for clergy", had initially been occupied by a heavily pregnant woman with two young children in tow. However, at one stop a saffron-robed Buddhist monk got on the bus and stood glaring down at her. Under his persistent stare she finally succumbed and relinquished the precious seat to the healthy young man. We were astounded by this and I was strongly tempted to say something to him, but in the end remained silent, feeling it was not my place to interfere.

• • •

"There is no boat. Not until these strikes are over."

After our island-long dash, the state of our tired, sweaty bodies and dust-caked clothes made this news doubly disappointing. Our informant, an equally tired and badly mosquito-bitten English youth, surveyed the group of twenty young foreigners sprawled about the deserted pier head with a nonchalant wave of his hand.

"Some of us have been here for days. There's only one Rest House, and pretty expensive at that. I slept last night in a temple courtyard over there . . ."

He lifted up his shirt, revealing a stomach more dotted with red marks than his face, and smiled ruefully.

". . . hence the bites."

"But is a boat expected?"

"Haven't a clue. Every official tells a completely different story. Main one is that the boat can't stock up on the Indian side due to the shallowness of the water, and it is only here that they have facilities. But, as the fuel and water is brought here by train, and there is a train strike . . ."

Another sardonic smile and a well-practised shoulder shrug told all there was to say.

Four days later a boat did come. From among the tight-lipped officials one hinted that it was a 'special' boat, sent over to collect a group of stranded Indian schoolgirls, and it was to be the last until Sri Lanka's present wave of labour troubles was settled – one way or the other.

Between Talaimannar Pier and India stretches a series of reefs, shoals and tiny uninhabited islands. Given the collective name 'Adam's Bridge' these 'stepping stones' appear in the great India epic, the *Ramayana*, when the monkey general Hanuman uses them to pursue the Lankan demon king Rawana when the latter kidnaps Princess Sita. Shades of Ulster's own Giant's Causeway, the legendary stepping stones built by the Irish giant Finn MacCool to aid his pursuit of his Scottish rival Finn Gall.

When the ferry finally arrived at the Indian port of Rameswaram the passengers were transferred to small boats to negotiate the last stretch of shallow water. There was a noticeable apprehension among the sizeable contingent of young travellers who had made the journey, for almost without exception they, like ourselves, were smuggling in a few kilos of 'Number One quality' cloves. We had bought ours in Kandy, after being told that cloves could be sold at a good profit in India. In a single backpack a few packages might have gone unnoticed, but even on the open deck the cumulative scent of so many kilos of concealed spices was pungently obvious.

And as we all trooped into the Indian customs shed, a motley bunch displaying little sartorial elegance, the distinctive aroma hung about us like a red warning flag. The customs officials began to sort people into queues, each queue leading to an inspection table. When Sheila was directed to a different table from mine, I caught the attention of the nearest official.

"Excuse me, can I go over there with her?"

He gave me a questioning look.

"And why?"

"She's my wife."

His face lit up with a massive smile.

"Ah – *you are married!* "

Such obvious pleasure at discovering a wedded couple among this dishevelled throng amused and surprised us. But it certainly worked to our advantage, for our gallant customs officer personally escorted us right past the tables before pointing to the exit.

"Go on through, please! And welcome to India!"

I took a quick glance behind me to see other travellers begin to empty the contents of their backpacks onto the tables. Oh well, all's fair in love and war. Within minutes we were once again engulfed in the deluge of noise, people, and posters proclaiming Mrs Gandhi's '20-Point Programme' that was India.

India (iii)

(11–27 January 1977)

We decided to take the train straight to Madras, a journey which saw us pass through 'Trichy' at 4am and ended with our arrival in Egmore Station at 4pm. Without too much searching around we found ourselves a dormitory room in a student centre, then set out to check for mail at the Poste Restante and see if we could unload our four kilos of Sri Lankan cloves.

At the shop where we finally sold them the owners made us sit for ten minutes discussing fake leather handbags while they observed a 'suspicious' character across the street. We wondered whether this concern was genuine or whether it was just a piece of staged melodrama designed to encourage us to part with our merchandise in their shop, at their price, rather than take it elsewhere. They need not have worried for we had little desire to hawk the packages around with us and were quite satisfied with the price offered. To our shoestring budget it certainly amounted to a good profit, and went some way towards reimbursing us for the money which had been stolen in Pakistan.

Madras, as was only to be expected from India's fourth largest city, was dusty, noisy and congested. Yet we did not find it off-putting – perhaps we were just becoming inured to Indian city life. Selling our cloves was far easier, however, than getting our student concessions for onward travel up the east coast – the railway bureaucracy took up a full four hours of our time. Nevertheless, we did not let this bother us unduly, another sign perhaps that we were also becoming accustomed to the Indian way of doing things. Anyway, there was little point in fretting with impatience, it would not have speeded things up in the slightest. I did not even concern myself with the fact that we had no 1977 stickers for our student cards – only when the old date eventually created difficulties would we bother to confront that problem.

There were other practicalities to attend to. Sheila had been suffering on and off from toothache for the past few weeks and she managed at last to get a filling. Our clothes were by now showing signs of advanced wear and tear, their former colours having long since been bleached out by the sun, so we included a visit to a teeming bazaar displaying an unimaginable array of inexpensive goods, and purchased a few replacement items for our wardrobe. At least they made our appearance just that little bit more respectable. We also visited the tourist office to obtain a 'liquor licence' each, available free to tourists and which were – so we had been reliably informed – highly sought after by rich Indians impartial to a bit of imbibing. We never did get rid of them.

These mundane matters were squeezed in around excursions to some of the temples for which the state of Tamil Nadu is renowned. Our first temple visit, however, was a nonstarter. Close to our lodgings, at least it had not required much effort to reach. We had just entered the outer courtyard when a temple official sitting to one side instructed us to remove our shoes, then insisted that we pay him a fee for looking after them. We duly complied but moments later another temple servant quickly approached and informed us that non-Hindus were not allowed in! Somewhat surprised but not wishing to offend religious sensitivities we retrieved our shoes and asked for our money back. To our astonishment, the shoe guardian announced that, although he knew we would not be allowed inside the temple, a refund was not possible. In this he was supported by his colleague who now loudly insisted that we leave forthwith.

Now, the money itself was quite irrelevant, but my willingness to accommodate religious sensitivities did not stretch to condoning blatant thievery, especially when accompanied by such aggressiveness, so I stood my ground and demanded a refund. The fact that a crowd quickly gathered seemed to unsettle the two officials and eventually we were given our money back.

But at the temples situated around the seaside village of Mahabalipuram, a two-hour bus ride south of Madras, we encountered no such distracting hassles. The varied assortment of temples here included freestanding structures known as *rathas* – massive boulders carved in the shape of temples or chariots; the dramatically-sited shore-temple whose outer protective wall was lapped by the waters of the Bay of Bengal; and, most intriguing of all, huge bas-reliefs in which entire rockfaces had been sculpted with a profusion of imagery. The most remarkable of these bas-reliefs, known as Arjuna's Penance, depicted an episode from one of the Hindu epics in an explosion of carvings, with a family of elephants stealing the limelight from numerous representations of Shiva. On the return journey to Madras our bus was so laden down with pilgrims that the tyres began to burn against the chassis every time the vehicle rounded a corner. Leaning over the seat in front, a beautiful child chatted away to us in basic English, calling me her "white uncle" and displaying not the slightest shyness.

Another day-trip took us to Kanchipuram, possibly south India's holiest Hindu city, a maze of narrow streets and feverish streetlife and completely dominated by soaring *gopurams*, the huge temple gateways. Then, in Madras itself, we visited the Kapaleswara Temple, dedicated to Shiva, its immense *gopuram* completely covered by a bewildering array of gaudily-painted stucco figures. To add to the spectacle, the Tamil harvest festival of Pongal was in progress and cows everywhere had been colourfully decorated.

For some reason the pressing crowds of people around the temple complexes never unduly concerned us, perhaps because each throng we were caught up in had a finite boundary, whether that boundary was marked by a turn in the street or an inner wall of the temple. But when we decided to visit a Tourist Fair in an extensive open-air setting we suddenly realised that the throng around us had *no* boundary, and that the tens of thousands of heads we could see in every direction were being added to each minute by hundreds more streaming through the entrance gates. There was no aggression, no unnecessary pushing and shoving, nothing to raise alarm – but we *were* alarmed. Indeed, we experienced a distinct panic at our situation, and when we had both been able to admit this to each other, we had no hesitation in making a dignified retreat. For the first time we had been scared and overwhelmed by India's multitudes.

• • •

Our train arrived in Puri just before midnight, a bad time to have to search out accommodation. When arriving late at night or early in the morning our normal practice was to bed down in the train station, but as this did not seem appropriate here we wandered the streets in a frustrating attempt to find a hotel which was open. We passed an office advertising tours of yet more temples, and stopped for a moment to peruse the notices pinned on the window. As I stood reading I realised with a start that a face within the building was peering out at me! Moments later a somewhat tipsy but quite friendly man opened the front door.

"You want to see Sun Temple?"

"We do. I see that there are bus trips from here?"

"Yes, yes. Very early in the morning. You must be here at six o'clock."

"Oh, we need a day to rest first. Then we will go on a trip."

"Okay, you go with my bus?"

"Perhaps."

He smiled and did not pursue the matter, reaching instead behind him to retrieve a bottle which he promptly offered to us. When we declined he smiled again and did not press us.

"Where you go now? No hotel?"

"We cannot find one."

He pushed open the door and indicated the floor of his office.

"You sleep here. No problem."

We had slept in far worse places. And in less reassuring company, for despite our host's inebriated state we had no fear that he would be a nuisance to us.

"Thank you, we will."

We entered the dark interior of the office, and although our companion again offered us his bottle, which we once again politely declined, he did not intrude as we got out our sleeping-bags but retired to the other side of the room where we heard him settle down on a straw-filled palliasse.

Puri, south of Calcutta in the state of Orissa, is one of Indian's premier pilgrimage centres, with a majestic temple over 200 feet tall celebrating Krishna as Jagannath, the Lord of the Universe. Although Puri attracts a constant flow of pilgrims, it is best known for one of India's most spectacular religious festivals, the Rath Yatra, when millions of pilgrims come to witness the procession of gigantic Jagannath chariots, pulled by thousands of devotees, and accompanied by elephants, along the town's main avenue.

Rath Yatra, unfortunately for us, is a midsummer event, but nevertheless thousands of pilgrims still thronged this holy centre, and, presumably in the hope that all the religiosity would manifest itself in charity, the streets were lined with the worst-looking beggars we had yet seen in India, many afflicted by terrible deformities or the effects of leprosy, and often in the company of deformed animals, the most startling of which was a six-legged cow – the two tiny extra limbs dangling lifelessly from its shoulders.

We took some local children to see *Bajbangmali*, a Hindi film of gods and goddesses, and it was a shock to see how overweight all the actors were – both heroes and heroines – in comparison to the ordinary man and woman in the street. Indeed, everywhere in India huge gaudily-painted billboards depicted Indian film stars as being chubby-cheeked and flabby-muscled.

Lord Jagannath's temple was not open to non-Hindus, and the only way to get a glimpse into the temple compound was from the top of the nearby library. But if the Sri Jagannath Temple was impressive, it had a formidable rival close at hand. We went on our promised bus tour to Konarak, the Temple of the Sun. There, standing alone amid the surrounding sand dunes, was one of the world's most unique religious structures, designed in the shape of a huge chariot, pulled by a team of seven galloping horses and having twenty-four wheels, each ten feet in diameter, spread around its base. Even more remarkable was that the façades of the temple were replete with beautiful carvings, many of them highly erotic, while every square inch of the giant wheels was encrusted with tiny but skilfully-executed ornamentations. A single-page leaflet published by the Tourist office gave as enticing a summary as any we found elsewhere:

> He is Surya, Sun God, riding the heavens in this magnificent chariot of stone. Speeding his sacred passage across the sky, seven great horses strain on twelve pairs of gigantic wheels, symbols of the sun's cycle. On a high parapet musicians celebrate Surya's procession through the day. Below, every living thing is gathered to attend his journey: kings and courtiers, warriors and children, women of surpassing beauty, lions and elephants, birds, flowers – and the naked image of lovers impelled by Surya's energy into a hundred postures of love and union. No aspect of live is unrepresented, no surface untouched by the vibrance of the sun. For at Konarak "this life is his eternal temple".

Our 'temple tour' was not finished yet, however. On another bus we went on a quick tour of the temples in Bhubaneswar. This quickness was not to our liking, but we discovered too late that the trip was geared mainly towards pilgrims, who were only given enough time to nip into each temple for a brief prayer. At some temples the guardians were again quite aggressive in keeping non-Hindus out, but at least we kept our shoes on.

• • •

Our stay in Calcutta remains something of a blur, partly occasioned by the apparent chaos of the city itself, and partly the consequence of our own pursuits. For a start it took ages to find budget accommodation. Then we had to search out air tickets to Thailand with a stopover in Burma. Next we had to locate the Thai and Burmese embassies, the Thai one being nowhere near where the travel agent said it was. Then followed a hassle to get our visas issued in time for the flight, a hassle compounded because our arrival in the city had coincided with two public holidays – a religious one quickly followed by a secular one, the Day of the Republic. Finally a quick visit to Calcutta's famous Jain temples, where our explorations were marred by the repeated endeavours of temple attendants to prise money from us. And, to cap it all, the noise from Hindu temples close by our hotel was deafening. Many makeshift shrines had been erected in the streets, all displaying highly imaginative, even grotesque, images made from papier mâché or sola pith. Most were the work of young people and students, and all in honour of Saraswati, the goddess of the arts and learning.

The day before we were to leave India, an evening stroll took us into an unfamiliar area of Calcutta, and we came across scenes of abject poverty, a poverty which the relative calmness of the evening allowed us to fully appreciate. This was one of the incongruous realities of India. We knew the poverty was there – indeed, it was the constant background against which everything else was judged – but because of the bustle and vibrancy of daily life, that was exactly where it often remained – in the background – and it was other images of India which predominated: the chaotic congestion of the cities; the dawn mist hanging over a slowly-waking village; the press of humanity swamping a train; the palpable energy generated around the sacred sites; the awe and the devotion inspired by the great temples; the constant demands made upon our senses by people, things, smells, noises, colours . . . We might be leaving India, but we had a feeling that India would never leave us.

Burma

(27 January – 3 February 1977)

The only way to enter Burma was by air; should anyone remain in doubt about that fact, capital letters at the bottom of their visa served as a prominent reminder: LAND ROUTE NOT PERMISSIBLE. The normal practice for backpackers was to make a stopover en route to Bangkok, and pick up the same flight at the same time one week later, the longest stay permissible. For visitors a week was a very limited period indeed in which to see an entire country and we tried to glean as much advance information as possible about distances, time taken to cover those distances, whether certain places were "worth visiting" – remembering that travellers often had very subjective ideas as to what was worth visiting and what was not – and whether any new locations had been 'discovered' which it was important not to miss. Hence, even as our plane touched down we already had our itinerary planned: arrive in Rangoon; train to Mandalay; riverboat down the Irrawaddy River to the ancient ruins of Pagan; return to Rangoon.

One thing we had also learned in advance was how to make the week in Burma relatively inexpensive. Because Burma gave such a poor official exchange rate – six kyats to one American dollar – most travellers, or at least those aware of the procedure, bought duty-free cigarettes and whisky before flying in. So, for US$23 worth bought at Calcutta airport, we received 780 kyats on the black market in Rangoon – almost 34 kyats to the dollar. This was an amazingly wide discrepancy; in other countries the black market rate was invariably a small percentage above the official rate, and often was not even worth the hassle involved. Everyone in Burma knew that this was a routine travellers' practice, but as long as you cashed two to three dollars at the airport to keep officialdom happy no-one asked how you proposed to live on so little.

And selling the goods posed no problem: hustlers accompanied us on the converted minivan taxi from the airport, the rate offered slowly increasing the nearer we got to the YMCA in Rangoon – the main budget accommodation for young travellers – and by the time we were disembarking outside the building we were simultaneously handing over our duty-free goods for the standard price. Some travellers held out until Mandalay where a marginally better rate could be obtained, but a long train journey could see a whisky bottle either broken or stolen, and we were content enough with our exchange.

Indeed, we were soon to discover that – for the first time on our trip – we had no need to economise, for we actually possessed far more money than we could possibly spend. However, our surplus kyats could not be reconverted at a bank because officially they did not exist, and the hustlers who pestered us so much to sell us kyats were to prove conspicuously absent when later we wanted the exchange to go the other way. But for now our concern was with making the most of our hurried week in Burma.

• • •

We spent our first evening in Burma resting up in the YMCA in Rangoon, chatting with the friendly staff and swapping travel anecdotes with fellow backpackers. The following morning we went to the railway station at 5am, to ensure that we would get seats on the 7am train to Mandalay – a thirteen-hour journey. Rangoon itself would have to wait until our return – then we would explore it at our leisure.

The prospect of such a long train journey, rather than being something which daunted us, was an opportunity we looked forward to with much anticipation, for we knew by now that there was no better way of gaining an introduction to a new country. The journey fulfilled all our expectations, and our only regret, as we encountered more and more of the good-looking, ever-smiling and hospitable Burmese people, was that one week in Burma was going to be far too brief.

During any lulls in our encounters with fellow passengers we surveyed the passing countryside, which was surprisingly flat, with the lush green of the rice fields frequently punctuated by the dazzling white of innumerable Buddhist stupas. When we finally arrived at our destination, instead of feeling tired we felt relaxed and contented. A reflection of the company we had been in, no doubt.

In Mandalay the next day we climbed Mandalay Hill. A total of 1,729 stone steps led up to the summit, nearly 800 feet above the surrounding countryside. The view from the top was magnificent, but the actual climb was just as fascinating, for the stairways were covered over and therefore cool even in the midday sun, and everywhere there were astrologers offering their advice or pedlars selling their wares. Small temples and statues also provided reason for pausing on the ascent.

Markets, like trains, are a good place to get close to the populace and Mandalay's main market was no exception, for it was thronged with people busily engaged in browsing and purchasing, many of them resplendent in their tribal costumes. We visited the same market in the evening, when part of it became the 'night market' – as the tourist brochures called it – although it would have been more aptly called the 'black market', as indeed some local people termed it. Never before in Asia had we seen such an array of smuggled goods, with stall after stall displaying any articles you desired – for a price, of course.

We would not be staying at our Mandalay lodgings for a second night and after another visit to the night market we journeyed by horse cart to the pier where the boat which would take us down the Irrawaddy River to Pagan was moored. The boat was scheduled to leave at 5am so we went on board hoping to find somewhere to lie down. However, many of the other passengers had the same idea and it was some time before we managed to stretch ourselves out on the deck. With so much movement around us we found it impossible to get to sleep.

• • •

As we made our slow progress down the Irrawaddy I surveyed the other passengers sitting on mats and scraps of material on the deck of this rusty old riverboat. Two saffron-robed Buddhist monks and six identically-clad young boys occupied the space next to us, the boys sitting quietly and demurely in the presence of the sober-faced adults, but at every opportunity giving us a surreptitious stare. I always smiled back when I managed to catch their eye, but they would immediately turn away, their faces all with an identically distant and impassive expression. Over to the starboard side a circle of women gradually ceased their animated conversation as one by one they lit up massive cheroots and began smoking with obvious relish.

Someone called out and heads looked up in unison. I pushed aside the canvas awning which was draped above and alongside us as a sunshield, to see the familiar gathering of people on the distant bank which indicated that we were arriving at another 'port of call'. These landing places were so in theory only, for the Irrawaddy, being a flood river whose volume varied with the seasons, could be quite a distance from the solid earth bank, and would-be passengers often had to traverse a wide expanse of mud. Once the boat had reached the 'shoreline' the crew would lower two planks onto this mud, one for disembarking passengers to run down, the other for new passengers to run up. At each stop girls carrying large baskets would find some way to sell their merchandise to the passengers, both sellers and passengers stretching their limbs to the utmost to effect these transactions. At longer halts the girls would be allowed to board the vessel while they made a speedy round of the passengers. When the boat was ready to resume its journey the planks would be splashed a few times in the water to remove the clinging mud, and with all those assembled on the shore smiling profusely – and the children for some reason all giving the 'V' sign – the boat would make its way out into midstream again.

• • •

After sleeping for a second night on board, we entered Pagan in the misty coolness of the early morning, and after a much needed shower in our lodgings set off to explore the extensive ruins which were arrayed in profusion on all sides. But a short excursion – in an attempt to escape the torrid midday heat – was impossible, and it was late in the afternoon before we returned, hot and dusty, but elated by all that we had seen. Here at last were ruins we could wander around unmolested, walking along dusty tracks deserted of people and vehicles, with no sign of a tout, a souvenir stall, a rush of inquisitive locals or pestering, prospective guides.

Pagan's golden age had been in the 12th Century, when it had once contained some 13,000 religious buildings – of which 2,000 still remain. It stands on a flat plain by the banks of the Irrawaddy; indeed, the changing course of the Irrawaddy has been responsible for the destruction of about one third of the original city. Once described as 'the most remarkable religious city in the world', it was still possible to experience a sense of its former magnificence, for everywhere we turned we were surrounded by temples and pagodas of every size. Often in Asia the bustle of humanity around a temple could distract from the structures themselves, but here in Pagan's splendid isolation there was nothing between us and the ruins but an eerie silence.

"You two look tired?"

The way we plonked down onto our chairs gave the Norwegian his answer.

"Did you buy any 'antiques'?"

I laughed, remembering the secretive way workmen, engaged in repairing those parts of the ruins damaged by the earthquake of 1975, had shown us 'real antiques', which had "been found after the destruction and hidden so that tourists could see them, and the government could not steal them all". We had remained completely sceptical about such claims, and later by accident had actually stumbled upon a workshop where such 'antiques' were being manufactured, then knocked about a bit before being finally rubbed in soil!

"No, did *you* buy any?"

"Of course not, but I might buy some gems."

I raised my eyebrows in surprise. Surely he was not going to risk money on this, the most common method of inveigling gullible tourists to part with their money.

"Come in here and see for yourself."

Following him into one of the bedrooms, we found two Burmese males already there, one of whom rose and closed the door behind us, then proceeded to fasten the window shutters. The dramatics begin, I mused.

The performance which followed was only too familiar to ones we had witnessed in Agra and Srinagar, and the Norwegian, despite undisguised warnings from the other travellers present, took it all in. "These gems are very precious." Of course. "They were stolen from a mine." Of course. "It was very difficult; they had guards." Of course. Before the deal was finalised we excused ourselves and quickly made our way outside. A group of children stood staring over the fence and we went over to them to say hello. Their faces lit up with more of those amazing Burmese smiles, the girls nudging each other and giggling shyly. As we laughed and joked with them I could not help thinking that here were the *real* gems, and no amount of tourist dollars could ever have bought such spontaneous warmth and innocence.

• • •

Our return to Rangoon was a somewhat hectic experience. After an early morning minivan ride to the regional centre of Nyaung U with its bustling market, we squeezed into an extremely packed bus for a two-hour journey to Kyaukpadaung. Next, a more luxurious ride on a lorry – lying on top of fertiliser bags – took us to the lakeside town of Meiktila, from where a final one-hour van ride deposited us outside the railway station at Thazi. We obtained seat reservations, but when we entered the carriage and located our seats it was to find them already taken. However, the occupants immediately got up and with friendly smiles insisted we take what was rightfully ours. We were glad to comply, for we were exhausted, though we did feel somewhat guilty. That guilt was compounded when our displaced fellow-passengers also insisted we share their food. However, everyone squeezed up tight while others found places on the floor, and in the darkened carriage we endeavoured to sleep sitting upright.

Our final day was spent wandering the colourful streets of Rangoon and visiting one of the architectural wonders of the world, the Shwe Dagon Pagoda. While the Shwe Dagon is actually a complex of numerous shrines and mini stupas, its most conspicuous element is its massive central stupa, which soars 300 feet above the surrounding countryside. It glitters like a huge beacon, hardly surprising as its façade is entirely covered with gold plates, and the tip of the stupa is set with many thousands of diamonds, rubies and sapphires.

It may have been a fantastic display of ostentatious religious extravagance – and I wondered whether this was really consistent with the 'middle way' recommended by the Buddha – but there was no doubting the Shwe Dagon's magnetic power and overwhelming grandeur. Sitting at its base engaged in friendly conversation with some local students seemed a fitting way to end our week-long dash through the socialist, Buddhist republic of Burma.

Thailand

(3–28 February 1977)

Our first full day in Bangkok was not an auspicious one. For a start, it was an unbelievably hot and noisy city. Indeed, Bangkok had the worst level of noise we had ever experienced – even in the privacy of our hotel room the traffic din penetrated and prevented us from sustaining a normal conversation. Perhaps we should have indulged in some leisurely sightseeing first, but Bangkok was the best place to purchase cheap flights from Indonesia to Australia and so we trudged wearily around the city until we found what we wanted. Indeed, we had almost given up when we discovered a suitable agent just as he was closing up shop.

Tired after this exhausting search we then retreated into a small restaurant hoping that a tasty rice meal would revitalise us, only to be given the worst food we had ever tasted, served by sullen and unfriendly staff. When we became convinced that part of it had once been on someone else's plate, for the first and only time in our lives we walked out of a restaurant without paying. The staff did not seem to care; they sat impassively watching us – probably wondering why it had taken us so long to leave.

During the day we had found many Thais, especially those employed in any type of official capacity, to be quite uncooperative. It was a shock to encounter such a situation, especially after having just left one of the friendliest countries in Asia. Were all Thais like this, we wondered. Was it anti-Western feeling, a legacy of the Vietnam war when American servicemen had inundated the city for R&R purposes? Or was it a reaction to the more recent incursion of hordes of foreigners whose only interest in the city seemed to be sex? As one drunken Western male said to us: "It's not Bangkok I'm interested in, it's bang-cock!"

The 'sex industry' was all-pervasive. Our double room possessed, for the first time in Asia since Kalam, a double bed, and we soon found out why – the hotel, like so many others, was frequented by prostitutes and their clients. If I had occasion to move around by myself within the building I was invariably involved in two or three separate propositionings. Many travellers were only too willing to avail themselves of these 'extra services', some of them treating the girls in quite a mercenary fashion, others going to the opposite extreme and pouring out their hearts to them in some shady corner. Yet, as the males got drunker, the expression on the faces of the girls could not have been mistaken for anything other than utter boredom.

On our second and third days we explored the fantastic Weekend Market, where we tasted a varied assortment of fruit we had never known existed; we visited the amazing Royal Palace, then Wat Phra Kaeo, and began to feel slightly more enamoured of the city. On a visit to the Temple of the Emerald Buddha, however, we were brought back to worldliness by a sign which read: 'Please do not point your feet in the direction of the Buddha.' Again I wondered what Siddhartha Gautama would have said about that.

We just could not warm to the city and decided to proceed without delay to the next stage of our itinerary – north to Chiang Mai, our springboard for a visit to the hill tribes in the Golden Triangle area. Even as we made ready to exit Bangkok, the city seemed to do all it could to hasten our departure. A shop assistant near the bus station tried to cheat us, and, made wary by this, I was quite alert when a few minutes later I bought our tickets at the ticket office. After the girl handed me my change I quickly calculated whether the price we had paid tallied with the backpacker's information sheets we carried. It did not. Indeed, either the prices had doubled in a year or we had just been swindled again. I immediately pushed my way back to the front of the queue.

"That's not the price of tickets to Chiang Mai."

Without any sign of embarrassment whatsoever the girl lifted up a nearby timetable, retrieved a couple of notes hidden under it, handed them to me . . . and then went on with serving the next customer. I stared at her, astounded by her brazenness. But I knew it would be futile reporting the matter to her superiors; something told us that they would have shown little interest.

Within a day of arriving in Chiang Mai we had discovered something which brought immense relief to both of us – there *were* friendly Thai people, after all. We excused their compatriots in the capital – large cities sometimes have a way of making people less approachable, less welcoming, more mercenary. We were now fully prepared to give Thailand a second chance.

• • •

While our stay in Chiang Mai was a welcome contrast to the noise and bustle of Bangkok – and we lodged at the relaxing Je t'Aime Guest House – we were impatient to visit the hill tribes further north. These hill tribes – a varied mixture of ethnic groups which had settled in the remote regions of northern Thailand – had numerous villages dotted over that jungled area known as the Golden Triangle, where the borders of Thailand, Laos and Burma met, and where much of Asia's opium was grown. The tribes we were visiting were admittedly reasonably accessible, for enterprising persons in Chiang Mai had been running 'jungle tours' for young travellers for some time. However, we did not avail ourselves of a guide, for we had been informed that independent travel was quite feasible.

The first leg of the journey was to Fang, where our evening was enlivened by a continuous stream of colourfully-dressed dancers proceeding past our hotel window on their way to a nearby temple, to the accompaniment of drums, gongs and cymbals. The following day we went by van to Thaton, having to hang on grimly to the back of the vehicle for part of the journey. Next we took an extremely narrow boat down the shallow Mae Kok river to Tamakaeng, from where, now joined by three other backpackers, we began our trek, in terrible heat, to the first accessible village.

• • •

"Ask him if he knows anyone who can take us to the poppy fields. I'd really like to tell people back home that I'd seen some opium poppies."

The others ignored the Canadian's request, probably thinking like ourselves that to be here, to be observing these tribal people, to be able to wander through their remote villages, was sufficient in itself and that the desire to indulge in 'checklist tourism' was an unnecessary distraction. So our questions to the headman of the Lisu village, where we were sleeping for the night, were of a more practical nature.

A villager approached our gathering just as dusk was falling, words were exchanged with the headman and we were beckoned to accompany the newcomer through the village – now with the distinctive smell of burning wood lingering over it, as the absence of a breeze meant that the trails of smoke emerging from vents in the huts were left to hang suspended like an evening mist.

Upon entering our host's abode he indicated the raised platform where we were to sleep side by side, and then, a broad grin revealing what remained of his teeth, he unearthed a small cup from its hiding place behind a roof-beam and pointed to the damp, resin-like substance within. We all took turns at sniffing the substance – raw opium – but no-one took up his offer. And before we all had our sleeping-bags rolled out and were ready to bed down, he was curled up on another platform – in that typical foetal position of the opium addict, his head supported by a hard wooden block – and puffing away unconcernedly through his water-pipe. At about three o'clock in the morning a noise awoke me and I raised my head to see our stumbling host rouse his teenage son, who sleepily but obediently set the pipe in motion again.

The next morning our party decided not to follow the rough map we had been given of the 'jungle tour' but to get off the beaten track – as far as that was possible. Our decision to do so was well rewarded. As we trudged up a hill which looked across into Burma we passed colourfully dressed villagers and were able to photograph the children by bribing them with sweets. Some armed hunters met us and their old flintlocks contrasted sharply with the brand new M16 carbine carried by a cheerful, English-speaking opium smuggler we encountered shortly afterwards.

Some of the villages possessed a simple but highly effective plumbing system: water from a stream above the village was carried through it via raised lines of bamboo piping which fanned out between the houses. When a household needed to make use of it they simply diverted part of the supply as it flowed past.

Our second night was spent in a Koumintang village, the third in an Akha village where the girls smoked pipes and wore highly ornate yet seemingly cumbersome headgear. The following day we were all suffering from blisters and badly in need of a wash. Then, just as we were surmounting yet one more ridge, the Belgian, who was leading, called back down to us.

"Chris, I think you'd be interested in seeing what's up here."

The Canadian, no doubt realising what was being referred to, unpacked his camera as he made his way, grinning, up to the rise, and a few minutes later any villagers passing by might have been amused at the sight of a party of Westerners photographing themselves in a field of white opium poppies.

• • •

On our return to Bangkok we lingered only long enough to acquire 1977 stamps for our student cards, with our 'magic letter' again proving its usefulness. Then followed an extremely crowded bus journey south to Prachuab Kirikkan, where we rested up a day before taking a night bus, on terrible seats, across a causeway to the island of Phuket. From there it was a simple ride by *bemo*, the local minivan, to Nai Hahn beach, where we discovered our own little bit of Paradise.

• • •

Nai Hahn beach was one of those places we felt would soon become numbered among the list of 'in' destinations beloved by backpackers, and we felt glad to have been there before it was inevitably spoilt. John, a laid-back and friendly local man, had constructed some rudimentary but quite exotic-looking facilities: a restaurant replete with bamboo seating and thatched roof, a few thatched accommodation huts which he called his 'bungalows', and some quite basic roof-only shelters. The food served up was wholesome and succulent – with a heavy emphasis on fruit – and it was also inexpensive. There was a small contingent of backpackers ensconced at the beach, augmented by a similar-sized group of local young people, and everyone was extremely relaxed and gregarious.

In the evenings we would all sit around a campfire on the beach, chatting, singing or simply gazing serenely out over the dark water. John passed around numerous chillums, "courtesy", he said, "of the management". There was a sense of international comradeship which was strangely reassuring. As I sat observing the interactions of those around me, I was reminded of a passage by Australian travel writer Peter Pinney, in which he described his encounter with an English girl who was wandering alone among the islands of the Caribbean, and of the night they sat on a beach while she philosophised about the benefits of shoestring travelling.

> "You're learning all the time," she went on. "You're continually exposed to new cultures, new ideas and philosophies, new attitudes to life. Education in the purest and best sense. There's a creeping paralysis of academic education trying to standardise everyone in the world, but you can learn to challenge it. We gain our learning out of books, but later begin to fear books because there are too many of them, and we give our lives into the hands of specialists. But, good heavens, if travel teaches you nothing else, it teaches you to think for yourself, to formulate your own opinions, and be self-reliant."
>
> We finished the bottle and threw it in the sea; the breeze was falling and soon the moon would rise.
>
> "There's thousands and tens of thousands just like me," she said in a low, earnest voice. "Young people, mostly, 'seagulls', travelling on a shoestring wherever they can go. Eager to learn, anxious to make friends, weaving a web of human understanding across the nations of the world. Young folk from every country in the world are on the move, almost as if they realised their elders had failed, and that now it was up to them. Internationalists, slowly wearing holes in closed frontiers, little termites eating away at nationalistic cults, each one carries with him the reflection of his country, plus a little understanding, plus a little hope, and takes it to new friends in foreign lands. It's not organised, it's not any kind of brotherhood, it's just a quiet and obscure social movement which seems to have grown and spread . . ."

Perhaps such sentiments sound naive and hopelessly romantic. Yet, although we realised that some of these 'seagulls' could be as mercenary and as irritating as anyone else, nevertheless sitting together at Nai Hahn beach, aglow with the hopes and dreams of youth, helped us believe in such sentiments, helped us feel those dreams could be made real. We just hoped that when we had children that they too would be able to feel for themselves that same togetherness, experience those same dreams.

• • •

A week was all that we could stay at Nai Hahn before we had to move on again. The evening before our departure we sat on the beach gazing upon the rippled reflection of the disappearing sun as it lightly caressed the surface of the water. John had taken us aside from the rest of the gathering, for he said he had something to tell us. We waited expectantly for him to speak.

"I did not tell you this before because you both look so happy here. I am being evicted."

"What!"

He did not look at us but kept his eyes fixed on the gently lapping tide a few yards below us.

"The restaurant . . . the bungalows . . . everything must be pulled down."

"But why?"

"I have no rights to the land. A big consortium is planning to build a modern hotel here, right beside the beach."

We felt devastated. It was as if John and his happy band of backpackers owned this beach and now rapacious businessmen were going to steal it from us. And yet it was more than that; when we tried to visualise a modern hotel sitting on Nai Hahn Beach we realised that a little bit of Paradise was soon going to disappear for ever.

• • •

We returned to Phuket to obtain onward transport to the Malaysian border. Local people directed us to the bus for Haadyai, and urged us to hurry, as its departure was imminent. During the dash along the busy streets my head smashed into an electricity box hanging from a lamppost and I was completely bowled over, my backpack pinning me to the ground like some upturned turtle. When we finally got on the bus it was to discover that there was blood seeping from a gash on the top of my head. Perhaps due to this I was sick twice into a plastic bag, though the route itself wound round and round innumerable hairpins which left Sheila feeling just as miserable.

The next morning we took the 6.30 train to Sungei Golok and from there walked across into West Malaysia.

Malaysia
(28 February – 28 March 1977)

The West Malaysian border town of Rantau Panjang was a small nothing-doing sort of place, and having just missed a train we had to wait three hours for a bus to Kota Bharu. We had entered Malaysia at the same time as a joint Malaysian/Thai army operation was being mounted in the border areas against Communist insurgents, and at one stage our bus was searched by Malaysian soldiers. However, their primary purpose was not to unearth insurgents but those smuggling rice from Thailand, where it was cheaper to buy than in Malaysia – or so a fellow passenger informed us, himself a smuggler. Our informant also told us that while the army posed a certain 'difficulty' to the trade, the customs men had all been 'safely corrupted' by his fellow smugglers.

We found the Malaysians to be hospitable, easy-going people. Once again a visit to a local market provided evidence of this friendliness, not to mention an opportunity to sample yet more foods totally new to us. For the first time since Europe we mixed public transport with hitchhiking, hopping slowly from fishing village to fishing village down West Malaysia's east coast. Driving was undertaken with much more heed to safety than in the rest of Asia and horns, thankfully, were rarely used. Drivers seemed only too glad to give lifts and many spoke extremely good English.

At Kampong Kuala Besut we took a ferry to a Government rest house, sited close to a fascinating fishing community and long deserted beaches with tantalising views of offshore islands. The waters of the South China Sea were the warmest we had ever swum in.

We hitched to Kuala Trengganu and on to Kuala Rompin, disappointed to find that the 'coast road' did not always run beside the sea. Indeed, at Kuala Rompin we had to walk for an hour to get near the water, only to find the waves too rough and the currents too dangerous to risk swimming. To compensate we went for a long walk along the shore but ended up with

133

our faces badly stung from the billowing sand.

Mersing was more to our liking although here we were to be at the receiving end of some very unwelcome attention. We had gone for a walk along the shore, collecting some of the beautiful shells which lay scattered in profusion upon the beach. At one part of the shore we were forced to scramble over a rocky outcrop. Unfortunately, in the process we disturbed a hornets' nest and were immediately and viciously attacked. As the incensed insects repeatedly dived-bombed us – their stings assaulting our flesh without respite – we fled in abject terror, unmindful of the jagged rocks which tore Sheila's flip-flops to shreds. When the hornets judged that we were either far enough away from their nest or they had exacted sufficient revenge for our intrusion, their attack abruptly ceased and we were left to take stock of our injuries. Sheila had come off worse, her face having been very badly stung – even at this stage one cheek had swollen so much she was unable to open her eye.

In terrible pain and still quaking from the ferocity and suddenness of the attack we made our way back to our lodgings. My fear was that the sheer volume of stings Sheila had suffered might quickly lead to complications. One of the hotel staff immediately dashed off to get some "special, hard to get" Chinese liquid remedy looking very much like iodine.

We felt like retreating to our beds to try and sleep off the experience, but the previous day we had chanced upon two backpackers travelling from east to west and we had arranged to meet up to swap information. We had been looking forward to this, for such encounters not only afforded travellers a pleasant opportunity to while away the twilight hours, but provided a vital means of gathering knowledge about the route ahead. So we kept our rendezvous, talking through our pain and with my voice, for some reason, slowly becoming weaker.

The following day Sheila's face was still badly swollen while my voice had completely gone. Was it all the talking last night, I wondered; was it a delayed reaction to the stings; or was it related to the shock I got when I saw Sheila's head hidden under a cloud of the ferociously attacking insects? The hotel staff again came to the rescue and gave me water sweetened with honeyed fruit, ordering me not to attempt to talk. Whether it was because of their remedy or the self-imposed silence, but after some twelve hours my voice gradually returned.

We hitched to Kota Tinggi and from there to Johore Bahru where we took the bus into Singapore. We had been told that long-haired males were not permitted to enter Singapore, and although my hair was much shorter than I normally wore it at home I dampened it down and tucked as much of it as I could inside my collar. There was no problem, however, and for the next few days we wandered around a city which, in certain parts, seemed little more than one huge shopping mall crammed with tourists.

On our return to Malaysia our route was now to be northwards, up the west coast this time. However, at Segamat we encountered our first real difficulty hitching and were stuck at our pitch for two hours. Unknown to us, however, a local Chinese youth, Andrew Chua, had been observing us and he finally came over, insisting that we accompany him to his home, where he and his girlfriend Josephine entertained and fed us. They took us out for a relaxing evening stroll around the town and insisted that we stay with them that night.

At the same pitch the next morning we were standing for barely a minute when a vehicle pulled in, and then we were on our way again, waving our goodbyes to our new friends and hearing them repeat their request that we return to Malaysia for their wedding.

Our lift dropped us in the centre of Kuala Lumpur where we checked into the official Youth Hostel. However, for some reason we found that our tolerance level for the noise of city life had worn decidedly thin and we hastily departed the following day, bound for the Cameron Highlands. In this refreshingly cool retreat – despite occasional downpours of torrential rain – we enjoyed numerous jungle walks, one an eight-hour trek during which an amazing variety of exotic butterflies bewitched us at every turn.

Then a few days were spent exploring the island of Penang before we took the twenty-five minute plane trip across the Strait of Malacca to Medan on the northeast coast of Sumatra, Indonesia's third largest island.

Indonesia

(28 March – 25 April 1977)

Long known to history as the fabled Spice Islands, the islands which comprise Indonesia constitute the largest archipelago in the world, with over 13,000 islands – of which 3,000 are sufficiently large enough to be inhabited – spread over 3,200 miles of sea. Given such a wide geographical dispersion, it is hardly surprising that this archipelago contains not only a rich variety of flora, fauna and landscape but of peoples and cultures. Thus, while Indonesia's population is predominantly Muslim, its diverse past is represented by the magnificent Hindu temples at Prambanan and the world's largest Buddhist monument at Borobudur, while its equally diverse present is manifest in the Hindu island of Bali and the Christian Bataks of Samosir. Samosir, our first destination, is an island within an island, nestling in beautiful Lake Toba in the north of Sumatra.

The ferry to Samosir left from Prapet and to get there necessitated an extremely crushed, stop-start bus trip from Medan, enlivened by three constantly giggling youths who requested that we give them an English lesson for most of the journey, amusing us with their preoccupation with knowing the English for anything connected with sex.

Even as the ferry approached Samosir we knew it would be a welcoming place, a feeling reinforced by the group of smiling children awaiting on the shore. One of the children immediately took us by the hand and led us to a lakeside abode, where an attractive young woman was washing clothes by the water's edge. She ceased her endeavours and greeted us warmly, explaining that she rented out rooms and inviting us to stay with her. After unloading our backpacks we went for a refreshing swim in the tranquil waters of the lake.

The days we spent on Samosir island were to be some of the most enjoyable of our entire trip. Undoubtedly, much of this was because we were treated by our hosts not as lodgers but almost as members of the family, and we would all sit each evening on a veranda thoroughly enjoying one another's company. Opening their house to backpackers was something new to the family and they plied us with numerous questions about what travellers might like, especially with regard to food. To our delight, they used our palates to test a succulent and exotic assortment of fruit dishes.

The people on Samosir, as in many parts of the highland area within which Lake Toba lies, are Bataks, a people who migrated from the foothills of northern Burma and Thailand over 1,500 years ago. For long their isolation allowed their animistic belief systems to flourish until German and Dutch missionaries in the 19th century converted them to a highly individual form of Christianity.

Their homes could be quite spectacular. Although our own abode was in the shape of a single-family house, many Bataks dwelt in large wooden buildings sometimes 60 feet long, in which different families lived in separate compartments – the whole structure raised off the ground on stilts, the space underneath being used for keeping animals. Most remarkable of all were the roofs, which were high at both gable ends and dipped in a graceful curve towards the middle. Unfortunately, corrugated iron sheeting was the material now most frequently utilised to cover the roofs, and its rusting and incongruous appearance greatly detracted from the otherwise extremely exotic-looking structure.

· · ·

When we left Samosir and returned to mainland Sumatra we took a bus to Sibolga on the west coast, then another to Padang Sidimpuan further south, many of the passengers on this second vehicle screaming in terror when it nearly toppled over on one particularly sharp bend. The family on Samosir had been so trustworthy it now came as a shock to find ourselves being frequently cheated whenever we tried to purchase anything, whether it was bus tickets or food from street stalls. Indeed, throughout the rest of our stay in Indonesia we were to encounter the most widespread practice yet of overcharging foreigners, with even Thailand falling into second place. In other parts of Asia poor street hawkers would sometimes try to add on a small percentage, and you could sympathise with them, although generally you were told the correct price, especially on public transport. But here much larger sums were involved, with everyone aiding and abetting each other in what proved to be an extremely widespread and constantly annoying practice.

For example, when we paid 2800 rupees for our bus fare from Padang Sidimpuan to Bukittinggi, we noticed the ticket-seller attempting to smudge over that part of the docket containing the price, and upon examining it closely we realised we should only have paid 2000 rupees. In annoyance we demanded our money back, a request the seller adamantly refused. Two passers-by came over to see if they could assist, and when they studied the tickets they pointed out that they were for a late afternoon slow bus, even though we had been assured they were for an early morning express bus, which we had specifically requested. It was just one rip-off too many, we felt, and although the seller initially refused us a refund we stood our ground and were finally successful.

The two passers-by, officials for an international aid project, informed us that they were on their way to Bukittinggi and so we made the bumpy journey there in the relative luxury of their jeep, our only concern being the driver's propensity to scatter any animals and humans who dared wander into his path. The fact that the only fatality was one unfortunate hen we attributed more to sheer luck rather than to his expertise behind the wheel.

When we next purchased bus tickets – this time for the journey from Bukittinggi to Lubuklinggau – we were extremely wary as we parted with our money. Everything seemed to be in order, however, and as a final question I asked the ticket seller how long the journey would last. "Oh, about twenty-four hours." Then he added, in a much quieter voice, "If it does not rain."

Sheila and I exchanged perplexed glances. What was that meant to mean? We were soon to find out.

• • •

"Not again!"

As the bus slushed through the mud I indicated to Sheila to look up the road ahead. There, about two hundred yards in front, we could see the back of a stationary vehicle, the first sign – only too familiar by now

– of yet another 'mud-hole' stoppage. Other passengers leaned forward, peering intently through the mud-bespattered windscreen and then they too slumped back against their seats with murmurs of despair. When we came to the inevitable halt a few moments later, most of the passengers, ourselves included, abandoned the vehicle with a well-practised resignation and went forward yet again to spectate. Anything was better than sitting impatiently in the stiflingly hot bus.

This time the queue of vehicles consisted of an equal mixture of buses and lorries, all awaiting their turn to attempt to traverse a mud-hole. These mud-holes – small craters would be a more correct description, as they were often over two foot deep – were formed when rainwater, collecting in pools on the road, caused the surface to loosen and each passing vehicle, aided by each downpour of rain, churned it up even more, until the former solidity of the surface had deteriorated into a muddy quagmire.

When we arrived at the top of the queue a bus was proceeding forward. It was obvious that it would not make it, but each vehicle's crew only accepted defeat when it was staring them in the face. Down into the hole the front wheels sank, but the rear wheels, having more to grip on, forced the front ones up and out of the hole. The crowd watched in a hush; this was always the tense part. Down into the hole went the rear wheels and slowly the bus inched forwards. Then the momentum ceased completely and sprays of mud rose in spitting arcs behind the vehicle as the rear wheels spun wildly. Time and again the driver revved his engine and each time the expectant crowd waited in hope for some indication of forward movement. But it was not to be and as the driver indicated defeat from his cab window, his three helpers – each bus had a crew of four: two drivers and two mechanics – squelched through the mud, opened a side compartment door and brought out the standard accessory gear of Sumatran heavy vehicles – two long metal stakes and a steel cable.

The stakes were driven in with sledgehammers a short distance in front of the bus and the cable ends secured to them. After much splashing through the mud, and often much digging under the buried rear wheels, the loop of the cable was connected to a special coupling on the rear axle and, using its own power, the bus slowly, inexorably, winched itself clear of the hole. While its relieved passengers returned to their seats again the crew retrieved

139

the stakes and the way was clear for the next vehicle's attempt. Yet within another few minutes the next bus would also be bogged down, often lying over on its side at a thirty-degree angle.

Sheila squelched her way over to me, mud caked up to her knees – our shoes, a useless commodity at a time like this, having been left on the bus.

"Let's go for a walk; I can't bear watching."

I understood her sentiments. While we had been on rougher journeys, the feeling that this bus trip could last indefinitely – and with no alternative means of transport available – was more than unnerving. On one occasion we had arrived at our place in the queue for a mud-hole at 8pm, and it was not until four the next morning that we had been able to move on. Then, we had hardly driven for fifteen minutes before we encountered another hole, though this only exacted a four-hour delay, as some of the more powerful vehicles managed to plough their way through at the first attempt. Then, barely half an hour after we had successfully negotiated *that* bogged-down position, we had been halted once again . . .

As we made our way along the line of buses to where a small crowd was gathered around a man selling home-made ice-sticks, preparing to yet again suppress any concerns we might harbour as to whether the water used was clean, a thickly-bearded and red-faced Westerner poked his head out of one of the glassless windows of a nearby bus.

"Hi! What'd you reckon?"

"I don't know. How many in front of you?"

I looked along the line and counted the vehicles.

"For you . . . maybe an hour and a half."

He sighed dramatically and passed this information to his female companion before leaning out again.

"Still, it makes it more interesting."

"You could say that, I suppose."

"Look at it this way. Did you notice those few hundred yards of solid road a few days ago – that token gesture marking the spot where you cross the Equator?"

I nodded affirmatively; it was at the commemorative pillar erected there that our jeep driver had insisted upon taking a photograph of us with our camera. "For your memories," he had explained.

"Well, soon it'll all be like that and people won't know what travellers like us used to moan about. I reckon we're the last generation who can cross Asia with any remaining sense of adventure. If our children come here they will find everything laid on – a 'Cooks Tour for Cheap Travellers', only it won't be that cheap. You came overland from Europe?"

I nodded again, holding on to the vehicle and endeavouring to free my sinking feet from the suction-like grip of the mud.

"Well, as I'm sure you saw, the influx of young travellers has led, even in the remoter areas, to the growth of budget hotels and rudimentary restaurants. But pretty soon the big boys will move in and push these small fry aside and in their wake will come increased prices, which will itself lead to the cheap travellers being squeezed out to make way for the international jet-set."

I agreed with him wholeheartedly and my thoughts returned to some of the places most at risk from such development: Band-i-Amir and its magnificent lakes; Nai Hahn beach and John's bungalows; even our idyllic location on Samosir island . . .

"Looks like we're moving up."

I moved to one side as his bus edged up one place in the queue. Strange how even a short advance could raise one's hopes of a speedy resumption of the journey.

Two and a half hours later *our* bus was finally on its way again, only to be halted twenty kilometres further on for two more hours while another queue waited to cross yet another river by ferry-raft – each vehicle having to be winched up the steep, slippery and disintegrating bank at the other side. And every so often more rain would fall, compounding the difficulties.

Fifty-nine hours after beginning the 'twenty-four-hour' bus journey from Bukittinggi we arrived at Lubuklinggau, sweaty and exhausted, for sleep had been impossible with the bus lurching from side to side alarmingly even on the better parts of the road. Our feet and lower legs were painfully swollen as a result of our enforced sitting position. We also discovered that our 4500 rupee fare had apparently only cost some local people 2500! Oh well, I guess it was worth it for the 'memories'.

• • •

After a full day at Lubuklinggau to rest up and allow the swelling in our feet and legs to subside we set out by train on the final stage of our journey through Sumatra. During the journey we again had to contend with a situation we were now well accustomed to – young people sitting themselves down beside us and requesting an English lesson. And this was not confined to public transport. In Bukittinggi and Lubuklinnggau we found small groups of young people waiting outside our hotels and no sooner had we emerged to go for a walk or search for food than we were approached with the inevitable request. Sometimes we conversed as we strolled along the street, at other times we would find some place to sit and hold our impromptu classes. It did get to be wearisome on occasion, especially if we were still physically tired from travelling, but we always tried to oblige. We felt that we were getting so much out of our travels, not to mention being constantly on the receiving end of so much generosity from people everywhere, that it was at least one way we could repay some of that hospitality.

Not everyone, however, was so willing to acquiesce with this constant demand for language lessons, as we were to discover on this particular train journey. Shortly after two youths had requested an "English lesson, please" and we had accommodated them beside us, another group of three youths entered our compartment and, seeing our backpacks on the luggage rack, immediately made their way towards us. However, on being made aware by our pupils that we were already spoken for, they smiled and waved to us before proceeding along the carriage. Unknown to us there were two young male backpackers further along and we heard the familiar "Excuse, can we have English lesson please?"

"Fuck off!"

The curse was so loud and so vehemently delivered that everyone in the carriage, including ourselves, immediately turned to look. The three youths stood there looking stunned and deeply embarrassed, while Sheila and I exchanged horrified glances, ashamed at such an ignorant response from fellow travellers. We beckoned the three youths back to our seats and somehow managed to squeeze them into our 'class', but for some minutes I could not continue with any lesson, so angry did I feel at the coarseness which had been displayed.

Why on earth did such individuals bother to travel abroad at all, I thought, if they had such a lack of patience with the people they were travelling among? It was not the first time we had encountered such behaviour, however, for we had met travellers who loudly complained that their "eggs haven't been boiled properly", travellers who reacted to local customs with visible derision, and even some who had no compunction about begging on the streets. We had assumed that all the hassles involved in travelling across Asia – the numerous vaccinations required, the tedious pursuit of visas, the heat, the endless bureaucracy, the language problems, the patience required to face the hundred and one daily problems – would have acted like a sieve, weeding out those who could not stomach such irritations and leaving a generally recognisable long-haul traveller, someone resourceful who could adapt to different circumstances and was prepared to make an effort to relate to local people. Not a bit of it, unfortunately. The backpacking fraternity was just like any other group of people and contained its share of the selfish, the rude and the arrogant.

· · ·

Shortly after being cheated out of another 200 rupees we took the ferry to Java. It was crowded with passengers, but eventually we managed to find a place to sit down, until a sudden downpour forced us to search out shelter. When we could find none we returned to our former location and just sat there in the rain.

We arrived at Merak where we boarded a bus for Jakarta; it broke down halfway there, as did its replacement – and once again the bus crew blatantly tried to cheat us – but finally we reached Indonesia's capital. We had no intention of lingering there, however – we would be returning in two weeks' time to catch our flight to Australia – and, anxious to visit Bali, we boarded a train for Jogjakarta.

We arrived in Jogjakarta at 7am, having had little sleep during the journey. Within a twenty-four hour period we had travelled by boat, bus and train and our tired, sweaty and dirty state was now compounded by a tiredness of will. Although we visited the Sultan's Palace our day at Jogjakarta was a languid and lazy one. We even decided against visiting the famous Buddhist monument of Borobudur, which was only an hour's bus drive away. It was a decision we were later to regret, but, although we had not analysed it at the time, after nearly nine months 'on the road' we were undoubtedly suffering from travel fatigue, possibly even culture fatigue. It was indeed an appropriate moment to be contemplating a break in our journey, for in Australia our intention was to settle down for a year and save money for the next stage. But first, the island of Bali beckoned and we intended to enjoy our time there to the full.

Kuta Beach, Bali, was beautiful. Not exactly paradise, for there were too many tourists about – real tourists this time, not just backpackers – as well as a large number of friendly but very persistent beach hawkers and a tide which was not the best for swimming. Indeed, the sea was more to the liking of the sizeable number of Aussie surfers who had taken up residence. These surfers were only ever encountered at two specific times of the day: heading *down* to the beach, surfboard cradled under one arm, and heading *back* from the beach when they had either exhausted themselves or the waves. Between surfers and travellers there was minimum contact, even when they resided in the same budget lodgings. It was surprising to observe how little both groups had in common; even at the end of the day there was no coming together when everyone – surfers, travellers and beach hawkers – gathered quietly on the beach to observe the stunning sunsets.

The touristic side of Bali was not so overwhelming that it hid the island's obvious attractions – especially its extremely relaxed atmosphere and the beautiful countryside with its luxuriant green mantle and the extensive rice terraces which utilised every available piece of ground. But the greatest attraction of all was Bali's friendly and ever-welcoming people, and we just hoped that increasing exposure to mass tourism would not eventually signal the beginning of the end of this emerald paradise.

•　•　•

All journeys inevitably have their end, and as we sat on the Thai Airlines jet waiting to fly from Jakarta to Australia, we knew that our journey too – or at least the first major stage of that journey – was coming to *its* end. I settled back into my seat and reflected upon the past nine months. They had been an unforgettable, exhilarating, often overwhelming nine months. Some old clichés were certainly applicable with regard to our journey: it had undeniably been 'the trip of a lifetime'; it had been 'a unique encounter with other cultures'; it had been 'a deeply enriching experience'. But others were more problematic. Had it really 'broadened our minds', had it enabled us to 'experience the oneness of humanity'? In a way it undoubtedly had, but we had started out with an optimistic belief in people anyway. Was there not an inevitability in that optimism being confirmed? Just before our departure an uncle had said to me, "If you believe in people you don't need to leave your own street to have that faith strengthened; if you *don't* believe in people, then going halfway round the world won't do a damn bit of good. People will always manage to find what they look for."

Ironically, the 'search for enlightenment', which made a journey to the East seem so attractive to young people in the late 1960s and early 70s, had played little part in our daily concerns. From the minute we stepped ashore on Asia we had experienced few esoteric musings and no preoccupation with developing our inner-awareness. We had simply taken each day as it came, soaking up every new experience to the full, and when thoughts intruded they were more often worldly, more likely to be concerned with how the ordinary people we travelled among managed to cope with the numerous trials and tribulations which so constantly beset them.

•   •   •

"We apologise, but would all passengers please leave the plane; we have a mechanical problem."

Seemingly Asia was not yet ready to release us. Back in the airport lounge we were informed that there was a fault with the plane's undercarriage and that a replacement aircraft would not be available until late in the evening of the following day. Until then – it was only 10.30 in the morning – all passengers would be put up at the Hotel Intercontinental at the airline's expense.

What a place to spend our last two days in Asia! Our room had its own *en suite* bathroom, with hot water and thick, comfortable towels labelled 'his' and 'hers'. In the grounds there was a heated swimming pool, while in the main lounge the staff wore smart, well-pressed uniforms, and waltzed around carrying drinks trays in their hands, napkins draped over their forearms. The group of dishevelled-looking backpackers among the passengers seemed completely out of place amid such surroundings. We were certainly made to feel so by the staff, who, just before dinner was served, disdainfully 'suggested' a meal which would fall within the budget agreed with the airline, rather than let us peruse the menu.

For the rest of that first day we luxuriated in this unexpected grandeur, frequenting the pool like children let loose on holiday or simply lounging in the comfort of our room, tasting a lifestyle which was as far removed as could be imagined from the one we had experienced over the past nine months.

• • •

As we relaxed beside the swimming pool and observed the other hotel guests – the paying guests, that is – my thoughts returned to an occasion when we had been sitting in a Delhi chai-shop in the company of other backpackers. Our attention had been drawn to a large coach which had just parked opposite, disgorging its load of Western tourists, all of whom – according to the consensus opinion of our gathering – we surmised to be middle-class, middle-aged Germans or Austrians. One of our group gave a dismissive laugh.

"That crowd'll not experience much of India from inside an air-conditioned coach. It's hardly worth their bloody while coming."

A few murmurs of agreement were voiced for this sentiment, but it was immediately called into question by one of our group whose extensive travelling accorded him a credibility which was beyond dispute.

"I know what you're implying, but I have to disagree. One of the problems with travellers is that they can easily develop a hierarchy. You all know what I mean: those who travel in their own vehicles claim that *their* experience is much more 'real' than those who travel cocooned on package tours; those who use public transport claim *their* experience is far more real that those who are isolated from people in their own vehicles; while hitchhikers and those who 'rough it' claim that *they* get closest of all. Each group down the ladder tries to establish that *its* way of doing things is more authentic than everyone else's, that the very hardships it subjects itself to is somehow a guarantee that it is getting closer to the heart of things."

He paused and looked around our small gathering, all of whom were now listening intently.

"I'm not denying that different modes of travel provide different opportunities for experiencing things, but it is also obvious that there are many people who are not open to that experience, *irrespective* of their mode of travel. To me, a far more important factor among travellers is their motivation. Take those tourists over there . . . noticing, by the way, that when we label others as 'tourists' we imply that we are somehow different from them – somehow *we* are not 'tourists', *we* are 'travellers'. But would the owners of this chai-shop, for example, see any real difference between our two groups, except that we spend less?"

Some of the tourists had wandered across the road, one man peering into the interior of the chai-shop to give our gathering a long, scrutinising stare, while others browsed at the nearby street stalls.

"As I said, take them as an example. Certainly you could say that travelling around in such a protective group, in an air-conditioned coach, was bound to make their experience less real. They'll never experience what travelling third class on a crushed Indian train is like; they'll never experience what it is like to be offered lodgings by some villager hoping to make a little extra income. But study them more closely. They all look as if they have children, mortgages, responsibilities. Are any of us burdened with such things?"

Heads shook negatively in unison.

"Furthermore, they all look as if they are more accustomed to genteel walks in the Alps or family camping holidays on the Italian or French Riviera. So what brings them here? Why should they decide to subject themselves to the many inoculations, the long flights, the heat and the smells, the hassles and the uncertainties? It would have been far easier going back to the Alps again this year. To come to Asia, I reckon that some of them must have said to their partners, 'We're missing something, we need to see how other people in the world live, we must go somewhere different.' "

The speaker paused again to survey our gathering.

"I really believe that *for them* to pick India rather than the safety of the Alps necessitated a bigger leap of imagination than was needed by any of us."

147

The faces around him evinced a growing understanding.

"How many of us had any hesitation in wanting to come to Asia, or faced any great dilemma over it? Well?"

That understanding was now complete.

"No, for us the decision to come to Asia, and to do it 'on the road' was easy. But for those people over there? I hardly think so. So can we fault them for the method they choose?"

He was right in so many ways. But just now, entombed within these four walls, I felt he was partly wrong. Barely twenty-four hours after finding ourselves stranded in the lap of luxury we were feeling increasingly claustrophobic, imprisoned by our plush surroundings. Apart from some of the decorative items strategically positioned around the hotel, there was little even to suggest that we were in Indonesia. We could imagine the same furnishings, the same carpets, the same staff, the same servile demeanour, in all the Intercontinental Hotels around the world. To stay at any one of them might have felt the same as staying at all of them. From the grounds we could not even see anything of life beyond the hotel perimeter – we could have been anywhere. Only the view from our bedroom window of Jakarta's massive Freedom Monument towering over the city and the array of different-coloured vehicles queued up in the main bus station far below afforded us a sense of place.

The staff were aloof and unfriendly – to us backpackers, that is – and our comfortable room began to feel more and more like an isolation ward. Our present circumstances might have been highly luxurious but so much more was lacking. There was no shriek of noisy children larking around the village standpipe. There was no host curled up opposite us sleeping off the effects of a night's opium. There was no local entrepreneur nosily chopping pineapples for the day's menu at his makeshift restaurant. There was no raucous throat-clearing as men in turbans greeted the coolness of a new dawn. There was nothing of this – only a spotless plasticity.

Ultimately it *was* the best way to finish our Asian journey, for it brought everything back into focus and highlighted just what we *had* experienced by the way we had travelled, what we would have missed if we had done it differently.

. . .

When we entered the customs hall at Perth airport we joined one of the lines of passengers queuing up to pass an inspection table. The inspections seemed quite cursory: perhaps a quick squeeze around a handbag, or a holdall zipper quickly opened, followed by a bit of groping inside, the zipper closed again, then finally a smile for the passenger to proceed. Our line kept moving forward at a reasonable pace, and there were only three or four people in front of us waiting to pass inspection when one of the officials stared over at me. He immediately indicated for everyone behind us to join another queue. Some demurred, for it meant joining a longer line-up, but he politely repeated his request. That was a bit of luck, I thought, to get into this one before it closed.

How naive can you be!

When it was finally our turn, one of the two officials standing before us indicated the full length of the table with a slow and somewhat dramatic sweep of his hand.

"Right, you two – EVERYTHING out."

There was something about his tone of voice and his officious demeanour which made me instantly recoil. I returned his stare for a few moments and then began to unload the contents of my backpack. Sheila did likewise and our belongings began to fill up more and more of the table – not that we had much, but when you set things down side by side it looks as if you are carrying more than you actually are. I glanced over at the former members of our queue; they looked relieved not to be still standing behind us and now understood the reason for our queue's sudden closure. Across from us another queue had also been closed, and another two backpackers were spilling their belongings onto a table.

As the two men inspected every single item, without any unpleasantness it must be admitted, but without any friendliness either, we began to feel increasingly uncomfortable. During our entire time in Asia most interactions with customs officials had generally been quite informal, even jovial. Now, having our worldly possessions handled and inspected this thoroughly by aloof strangers was akin to that feeling experienced by anyone who has ever had their home burgled – that disturbing sense of intimacy violated. If we had just been departing for a two-week holiday and our belongings consisted of neatly-pressed clothes, suntan lotion, a few guide books and whatever, then it might not have seemed so personal. But coming to the end of nine months' rough travelling with our backpacks filled with the odds and ends accumulated during the trip, or that bundle of clothes still awaiting a wash . . . there was something humiliating about it all.

Sheila was clearly feeling the same as I was – I could tell by the look on her face – and she soon articulated her disquiet.

"Can I ask whether we would have been asked to empty out all our belongings if we had been carrying smart new suitcases?"

The official glared at her with barely concealed disdain.

"Look, when we get young people arriving here from Asia, with their long hair, their rucksacks, their hippie beads, then the rule of the game is . . . EVERYTHING out."

Without even waiting to see how Sheila might respond to this, he resumed his careful examination of our belongings.

We did not mind these searches in principle. We understood the need for them. What was so objectionable in this case was the attitude displayed by the officials and the manner in which their task was being pursued – it was as if, simply because we were backpackers, we were presumed guilty until proven innocent.

The last time we had experienced such a search had been on our return to the United Kingdom from Amsterdam. Having lived there for over a year we had accumulated a fair amount of belongings – including a guitar, a cassette player, books, clothes – not to mention presents for everyone back home. We had travelled to England by boat from Hoek van Holland to Harwich, and as we passed through customs we had noticed the official stare intently at our passports, but paid little heed to it. As he handed them back to me and waved us on, out of the corner of my eye I saw him beckon another man over to his desk. Again, we thought nothing off it and continued walking, heading for the nearby train platform along with the other foot passengers. Then we heard someone call out:

"Could you stop there a minute, please!"

There was just something about the command which told me that it was being directed at us. We halted as a man ran up beside us.

"Could I have a look at your passports, please?"

I exchanged a surprised glance with Sheila before offering him our passports. He perused them carefully.

"Ah, right . . . you are not Mr Johnston, by any chance?"

Was this some sort of joke? Was this character an idiot? I stared at the man, perplexed.

"Afraid not. I'm the same person as named in the passport."

He attempted a weak smile, then cleared his throat somewhat embarrassedly.

"Of course, of course. Sorry, I just thought you might be someone else. There you are . . . you may continue."

As he had walked away from us Sheila and I stood looking after him, totally dumbfounded.

"What on earth was that about? Was he a policeman?"

"Presumably a plainclothes detective."

"What did he want?"

"Haven't a clue. Maybe because we seem to be the only ones from Northern Ireland on the boat it's got them all excited."

Still shaking our heads in bewilderment we had continued on our way to the train platform. The train was packed and although we managed to find seats it was quite a struggle to find spaces for the backpacks, the guitar and our assorted plastic carrier-bags and packages. But finally everything was stored where it would hopefully not annoy other passengers and we relaxed into our seats.

Some five minutes later I suddenly became aware that other passengers were pointing to some commotion on the platform outside our carriage. I looked out to see a man running past our window, gesticulating to two others following behind, who entered our carriage from the rear while he entered from the front. Even at that stage I was still innocently wondering what could be happening and it was only when our friendly detective stood in the aisle staring down at us that I accepted that we were the focus of their attentions. I glanced at Sheila, to see her eyes wide with amazement. What the hell was going on!

The detective leaned forward and looked hard at me.

"How long have you been out of the UK?"

"Over a year."

"Are you aware that The Prevention of Terrorism Act has been passed?"

What on earth is happening, I wondered. Act nonchalant.

"Sure you lot are always passing laws; it's hard keeping up with them all."

Irritation creased his features. Wrong move! Change tactics. Forget about acting nonchalant, or smart – act polite.

"I must ask you both to accompany me back to my office. Could you now leave the train."

Leave the train! After the struggle we had just gone through to store away all our baggage! He must be joking!

"No chance."

"What!"

"I said 'no'! It took us bloody ages getting sorted out here; we're not moving now."

His face went red and he fumbled for words; whether due to surprise or anger, we could not be sure.

"I am asking you to get off this train *now*, and accompany me!"

"And I'm telling you that we are not moving until you explain to us why you seek to detain us."

"We will not discuss that here."

The proverbial pin could have dropped, for every single occupant of our carriage was completely mesmerised by this little drama. Sheila nudged me.

"We'd better do as he says."

Our detective stood back a bit, waiting. But I was not ready yet.

"On one condition."

His eyes flared.

"Condition! I am ordering you . . . *what* condition?"

"This train is just about to leave, so we'll obviously miss it. We will do as you say – if you guarantee us *reserved* seats on the next one."

He stared hard at me, taken aback. While his brain worked at computing this request I looked around at the other passengers. For one ludicrous moment I felt like encouraging a little audience participation, by asking them whether they thought I was offering a fair bargain. However, I had no need.

"Okay, okay. Now please . . . off the train!"

And so we gathered together all our bundles again, smiled apologetically at our fellow passengers and began to make our way along the carriage, following close behind our captors. Just as I was about to descend onto the platform an elderly woman endeavoured to climb up into the carriage and I stepped back to allow her to pass. The sudden look of panic on our detective's face when he momentarily lost sight of me sent a chill coursing through me. These people are deadly serious, I thought to myself, we will have to tread carefully.

Although our escorts offered to carry our backpacks and other baggage, we declined, a decision we soon regretted for we had quite a walk to reach the detective's office. But finally we entered it, a medium-sized room with a large table in the centre, a few grey-metal filing cabinets against the walls and a second door leading elsewhere. There were three men involved in what followed – our detective, a somewhat taller colleague and a third man who for most of the time remained seated at the back of the room.

A space was cleared on the table and, item by item, our belongings were all arrayed before their gaze. The two detectives examined each object with care and attention: they held up the guitar, shook it, then peered inside the sound-hole; chocolate toys – for which the Dutch are famous – were inspected and sniffed; books were turned upside down and the pages flicked back and forth; audio cassette cases were opened and the cassettes rattled about . . .

At first we sat impassively, watching it all in some amusement. Being innocent we could afford a sense of superiority, waiting smugly for that moment when we could say "we told you so". But within minutes all that was to change.

First of all, upon emptying out the final contents of my backpack, two rolls of industrial strength adhesive tape fell onto the table and the looks which were exchanged between the two men registered with pinpricks of shock. The taller man held up one of the rolls of tape and stared at me, his brow creased with seriousness.

"And what is this?"

Five minutes earlier I might have told him that it was a plastic bucket in disguise, but not now, my former assuredness had received a jolt.

"Tape."

"Where did you get it?"

"In Holland I worked for Honeywell, at their distribution warehouse near Schipol airport. It's used for sealing parcels. I took a couple of rolls."

"What for?"

"We have hundreds of books back in Belfast. We are off round the world soon and want to box them all and store them with relatives."

They looked at each other, then over at the third man, but he just shrugged his shoulders. They resumed their inspection. Our pile of second-hand books, which had earlier been offhandedly piled up, now received a more intent perusal.

"Ah-ha – Brendan Behan's *Confessions of an Irish Rebel.*"

This time the looks exchanged between the two men seemed more assured, as if parts of a jigsaw were slowly falling into place. Or was I only imagining it, was I becoming paranoid? With a start, I then remembered that one of the books still to come before their scrutiny was *The Nihilists*, which included photographs of the great Russian anarchist Mikhail Bakunin and illustrations depicting the assassination of Tsar Nicholas II. Any confidence I had started out with now began to ebb rapidly away, and I could easily imagine how these policemen might manipulate their 'circumstantial evidence': rolls of tape, "such as is used for making bombs, m'lord"; the biography of a former member of the IRA; a book about anarchists and bomb-throwers. Who would believe how innocent it all was? I suddenly appreciated as never before the plight of people caught up in such circumstances.

The detective lifted up the book, perused the title on the spine – luckily it was a plain hardback bereft of its illustrated slip cover – appeared a little perplexed . . . put it down and lifted the next book! My exhalation of breath must have seemed quite audible. Thank Heavens for a policeman with no understanding of political philosophy!

Soon my confidence began to return, for the tall detective seemed to have realised that his colleague had been overzealous in detaining us and he began to look increasingly bored with the proceedings. Our diligent detective, however, had still not given up hope. He went over to one of the tall filing cabinets, opened the door and lifted down an oblong cardboard box. He carried this box over to the table where he slowly opened the lid. Inside was an object enveloped in clear polythene wrapping. The detective carefully removed the polythene to reveal a hand-held metal detector. For some reason, a sense of politeness had returned to him.

"Do you mind if I run this over the outside of your clothes?"

"Go ahead."

And so the metal detector was moved slowly over our bodies, and finally, for good measure, along the outside of the guitar. Then the detective carefully wrapped the polythene around his precious gadget again, replaced it equally carefully in the cardboard box, and finally returned the precious box to its place in the cabinet. Do I laugh or do I cry, I thought. But I did neither, for our last scare was about to hit us.

"And what's this, then!"

I could not believe my eyes! I had seen the tall detective reach his hand towards our possessions and to my utter astonishment now saw him lift up a hypodermic syringe! How the hell did that get there! My mind swirled in a panic. I was convinced he had nothing in his hand when he reached over, so how did it get there!

"Well?"

His stare was malevolent now, his look self-satisfied. It must be a bloody plant; the bastards are intent on stitching us up! My mind was still in a swirl when suddenly the third detective, still reclining at the back of the room, gave a low laugh.

"Oh, that's been there since the last boat. Must've rolled down the table."

Our relief was immense. Yet it was tempered by a realisation of just how easy it would be for these people to frame us. The sooner we were out of there the better.

The discovery of the syringe had the effect of removing the tall detective's last remaining interest in us. He pushed his chair away from the table, still holding the syringe in his hand. Occasionally he would sniff at it and mutter to himself.

His colleague, now looking a bit sheepish, finally indicated that we could repack our belongings. His last hope, it seemed, was the telephone call he was awaiting, for earlier in the proceedings he had gone into the adjoining room to phone through our details to someone. But when his return call came through, his last chance was also proven negative. He smiled and attempted to be light-hearted.

"There are your passports back. I see from yours, Mr Hall, that you were in France in 1968. Were you on holiday?"

I knew we were not completely free from the clutches of these people, but I wanted to depart on an air of confidence.

"I was in Paris for the revolution."

He stared at me, then managed a weak smile. Perhaps his intentions all along had never been to create any hassle; perhaps he was simply watching his back, worried in case a superior might accuse him of letting two Belfast 'terrorists' slip through his fingers.

"I'll walk you back to the train now. I apologise for detaining you for so long."

Back at the ticket desk the detective identified himself to the girl behind the counter and we heard him asking for reservations. The girl began to demur, but he repeated his request more insistently and she speedily complied. He handed us our tickets and bade us goodbye.

When we boarded the train we realised what the girl had been about to say: there was no need for reservations, for there were only four other passengers in our carriage! We settled down for the journey to London in a relieved but sombre mood.

And now, as our examination at the hands of Perth's customs officials continued, Sheila continued to fume and attempted one last intervention.

"I reckon that if this is the way you select passengers for checking, then the best way to bring drugs in would be *not* to have long hair, *not* have rucksacks . . . you could obviously get through much quicker that way."

This time the stare was malevolent, the mask of disinterested professionalism had been momentarily displaced.

"And if you kept any further comments to yourself, *you* could get through a lot quicker too."

Welcome to Australia!

Australia

(26 April – 31 October 1977)

"You two are in for a few surprises."

I paused in my perusal of the well-thumbed Situations Vacant page of the communal copy of the *West Australian* and stared across the table at Joe, the talkative Englishman.

"We're listening."

Buttering himself another slice of bread – bread, jam and baked beans seeming to be the favourite diet of travellers in this Travel-Mates hostel in Perth – Joe indicated with a wave of his hand the other three persons present.

"Wolfgang's been here three weeks without any sign of work. Erich and Ursula even longer. I've only had two days' work myself – and I've been here eight weeks."

I exchanged a doleful look with Sheila.

"Second surprise coming up. While you were crossing Asia, like us you probably heard stories from other travellers about the fantastic wages to be earned here? What was the figure you were told?"

I did not need to think too hard – the topic was already foremost in my mind.

"Some people claimed you could save $1000 a month."

"Well, the average basic wage, for unskilled work, is $130 a week. Those big bucks only come after working aeons of overtime in the mines up north, and Aussies indulge in an orgy of overtime that would frighten British workers. And don't count on getting your work visas renewed either; two girls with good jobs were refused an extension last week."

This was indeed disappointing news. My mind swam with hurried calculations. Would it now be possible to save enough on a one-year work visa to finance the flights to, and the high cost of living within, the countries on the second leg of our itinerary – New Zealand, the South Sea islands,

Canada and the USA? I glanced again at Sheila; she too looked miles away in reflection. I returned to my perusal of the newspaper columns. Well, we could only wait and see. Little did we realise that within a year we would be setting foot on mainland Asia once again.

Looking for work proved to be a frustrating task. For the next few weeks we trudged from office to office, industrial estate to industrial estate, without success. It was reminiscent of our search for work in Amsterdam, only here there was no language barrier to explain away our daily failure. And all the time our savings were being inexorably eaten into. For a short period I got a job at a brick factory loading an endless supply of bricks onto pallets. Until then I had never realised bricks could come in so many different shapes and sizes, and with so many variations of roughness, each having its own unique way of assaulting the skin. Despite wearing heavy-duty gloves my hands became so cracked and dry they felt permanently like sandpaper. But that work soon came to an end – not that I was all that sorry – and my search began all over again.

I was so concerned by this lack of success I visited a downtown social services office, to investigate employment possibilities on the strength of my degree in Social Studies, although I was careful to point out to the receptionist that I only had a one-year work permit. The man who eventually interviewed me was welcoming and enthusiastic. He strode purposefully over to a large map of Perth and proceeded to outline the different departmental responsibilities within the city, then began to describe what opportunities existed for someone like myself. It was with difficulty that I managed to halt him in mid-flow and remind him of my one-year residence restriction. It was of little avail, for he resumed his fulsome presentation of Perth's social services provision and indicated where, after training, I might find a role within it.

Had he not understood me, I wondered? Or was it easier than I had imagined to circumvent the one-year limitation? During my next opportunity to intervene I said I felt it would be wrong for me to accept training knowing that I would be departing before it could be properly utilised. But he continued regardless, outlining the wages – which he admitted would not be that great at the beginning – and the gradual employment route that I would have to follow. Then, for some unknown reason, he began to paint a somewhat less attractive picture of the work possibilities in Perth, and as he did so he moved across the room to another map, this time showing the whole of Western Australia.

"However," he said quite dramatically, "if you were to consider working way up north, then . . ."

To my astonishment he now outlined employment possibilities far in advance of what was apparently available in Perth – a shorter training period, a much higher pay scale, access to a plane, and a host of different responsibilities, including acting as liaison officer with the Aboriginal communities . . .

Later that day one of our fellow hostellers offered an explanation.

"It's so hot up north, the government can't get people to work there. As far as I know – and I'm surprised he didn't tell you this as a further incentive – those who work above the 20th parallel can claim all their tax back."

I did not avail myself of the offer, however. Something more suitable was bound to turn up soon, I convinced myself.

And something did turn up. For Sheila it was a job as housemaid in the Sheraton Hotel, a job which she was to keep for the duration of our stay in Perth. I searched on for a further week and finally turned up a job at a factory making asbestos sheeting. I took this job with some trepidation, for the dangers of asbestos were then beginning to be widely publicised. However, I was to leave within a few months, not because my concerns finally made me terminate my employment, but because it was terminated for me.

The workforce was composed of different groupings, but two stood out because of their disparate attitudes to work. The first comprised those who were either recently arrived immigrants or first generation Australians who still identified with their immigrant roots rather than felt themselves to be 'Aussies' – Italians and Poles and others. Another was made up of young 'pure-bred Aussies'. The first group worked hard and conscientiously, a primary goal in life seemingly the amassing of savings as quickly as possible. Management did not even have to ask this group whether they wanted to work overtime or not. The second group, however, could not have been more of a contrast. When they did work they worked well, but they also had a

159

proclivity to work hard at avoiding work, constantly dreaming up schemes to escape the factory grind from time to time, whether that entailed a few hours in the middle of the working day or a few days out on the sick.

These young Australian workers felt there had to be more to life than sweating on a factory floor, and filled their weekends with drinking, 'chasing Sheilas' and speeding around in their cars – except for the few who were surfing fanatics. They got paid on a Friday but were invariably broke and scrounging off each other by Tuesday. When they wanted a break, or often just needed an outlet for their frustrations, they resorted to sabotage. This practice took numerous forms. Sometimes small bits of metal would be dropped into machinery, bringing whole assembly lines to a grinding halt. At other times the sabotage was more dramatic: during one night-shift a short length of bare wire with weighted ends was flung up at overhead electric cables and the resultant short-circuit plunged the entire factory into darkness for hours. Two of these young Australians spent ages rehearsing how they might break a leg by falling in front of the heavy trolleys which ran along the factory floor on track-lines – so that they could then submit an injury claim – but thankfully this highly dangerous stratagem was never put to the test.

This personal revolt against the work ethic and factory life did not stem from any conscious political radicalism; the views these young men held were either completely apolitical or often quite reactionary. I did what I could to make them desist and at times actually managed to thwart their more outlandish escapades, but I did so with a certain amount of guilt. It was okay for me, I reasoned, to want to work hard – I had a purpose in being here, I was saving money which would allow me to see more of the world. But what was on offer for them? They seemed to have little prospect but a long tedious life on the factory floor. For all their Aussie bragger they appeared – compared even to unemployed and disillusioned youth in Ireland – profoundly rootless and their primary focus in life seemed to be centred around an endless pursuit of hedonistic activities in the sun and the avoidance of unnecessary responsibilities. As someone complained to a national newspaper at the time, the real cultural symbol of Australian youth was fast becoming the discarded ring-pull of a beer-can.

The foreman with responsibility for our section, an extremely likeable immigrant from Poland who always tried to be understanding to these young workers, was at his wits' end and I felt extremely uncomfortable at his predicament. He knew that I was endeavouring to advise wiser counsel, but there was little either of us could do to counteract these destructive manifestations of alienation and boredom. Matters finally came to a head one shift when a spanner – literally – was thrown into the works and an entire section of machinery ground to a halt amid a flurry of angry and gesticulating management. The next morning, to no-one's surprise, our whole shift was paid off to a man, and as we made our way out through the factory gates for the last time I looked back to see the foreman standing alone, forlorn and with eyes downcast. It was a sad situation for all of us. I was now without money again – but I consoled myself with the thought that at least I was no longer breathing in asbestos fibre, and indeed, because of the worries it later gave rise to, I have often regretted not having got the sack sooner.

Luckily I soon picked up another job – working at the Swan Brewery, named after the Swan River which runs through Perth, and alongside whose bank the brewery was sited. The brewery was then housed in old premises, though it was preparing to move into modern ones. Because most of the jobs were quite monotonous – and no doubt because such monotony could affect both efficiency and safety – an unskilled worker like myself changed jobs every 45 minutes. I might start my day packing loaded boxes onto pallets, then move to the bottling area to ensure that bottles were not jamming up the long conveyor belts – wearing ear muffs to deaden the unearthly din of so much clinking glass. Following that I might find myself sitting before a luminous screen observing a line of cleaned empties trundling past, looking for the tell-tale signs of cracks in the glass. My favourite job, however, was driving forklift trucks around the loading bay.

Every three job changes you were permitted to go and collect a free beer and for the first few days I availed myself of this perk. However, not being overly fond of drink the novelty soon waned and I stopped, much to the surprise of my Aussie workmates, for whom this perk was extremely popular.

But for some workers even the free beer was still not enough. In the noisy bottling area the workers had their own system of sign language by which they passed on warnings to those who were guzzling beer – warm beer at that – taken directly from the conveyor belts. Two fingers urgently tapped against the upper arm – symbolising a corporal's stripes – signified that one of the foremen was on the prowl. The miming of an imaginary glass being lifted to the mouth indicated that the danger had passed and drinking could resume. I watched in disbelief as one worker, completely drunk, sat before the luminous screen and lifted every fifth bottle out of the line – whether it had a crack or not – only to fling it over his shoulder where it splintered into pieces on the ground. During one evening shift two of the workers in the loading bay were so intoxicated they repeatedly crashed their fork-lifts into the steel supports of the raised platforms upon which the tiers of full pallets were stored. I spent the shift in constant dread that an entire section would come crashing down upon my head.

I had cause to visit Perth General Hospital during my stint at the brewery, when I hurt my back lifting a large barrel. The doctor seemed strangely pleased when I told him my problem.

"It's good to see someone from the brewery coming here with a *different* complaint."

Seemingly he and his colleagues were exasperated by the predictable catalogue of drink-related problems prevalent among the brewery workers, which ranged from the physical – particularly liver damage – to the psychological and social, especially marital difficulties.

The brewery management, perhaps because of this negative public image, were actually proposing that when they moved to their new premises the free beer perk would cease. I attended a mass meeting of the workforce and heard union leaders outline areas of concern raised by the move. The issue of free beer was not mentioned, of course, but it was quite obviously part of the hidden agenda.

And while I was moving between jobs Sheila continued as housemaid at the Sheraton, filling her day with a routine which became almost second nature. As soon as she entered a room – assuming the occupier was not in residence – she had to strip the used sheets from the beds. The beds were not to be remade at this stage, however, being left to air. Instead, she would proceed to the *en suite* bathroom where she removed the used towels and any rubbish left by the occupants, before giving it a thorough clean, toilet and shower included. New towels were hung up . . . in a specific fashion.

New packets of soap were left . . . in a specific place on the washhand basin. The glasses used for holding toothbrushes were cleaned and left . . . in a specific place beside the soap. Back into the bedroom now to put on clean sheets, with the bedspread left hanging . . . in a specific way, of course. New sachets of coffee, milk and sugar were deposited beside the coffee maker. Then it was time to dust and vacuum the room, and finally the carpet pile was raked to make it sit up straight. A final check to make sure the curtains were also hanging in the correct manner and it was on to the next room. Each housemaid had their own floor – Sheila was on the 12th, which had twelve rooms.

While the work was repetitive it was not unduly trying, the main drawback being that Sheila only met her fellow workers at break-times, except for the occasion when Perth felt the tremors of a distant earthquake, and as the 12th floor swayed and coat-hangers tumbled noisily inside a wardrobe she prudently fled to join the rest of the staff. However, this respite only lasted ten minutes before management deemed it was safe for everyone to return to work again.

• • •

As Sheila closed the door of our flat and began to remove her jacket, I looked up from my reading.

"Well?"

"It was positive. I'm pregnant."

Although the fact that we were going to be parents was unplanned, we were nevertheless delighted. It did pose a few problems, however, the main one being that our original plans for a round-the-world trip had to be abandoned. Our Australian friends urged us to remain in Australia, and the friendly staff at the prenatal clinic said they would write to the immigration department supporting an extension of our work-visas. We were not sure whether they were being realistic about this – we imagined that getting pregnant must be a well-practised ploy to try and circumvent immigration law – and anyway we were deeply undecided about whether we wanted to stay or not. It was only to be much later, back home in the midst of yet more of Ulster's horrendous butchery, that we began to wonder whether we should have given the matter more serious consideration.

Eventually, we decided that it would be best if our child was born in Ireland. Even if we gained an extension to our work-visas it was most likely to be short-term and we could find ourselves having to resume our travels with a toddler in tow. Also, although we had wanted to escape from Northern Ireland and its conflict for a while, we had never intended to run away from it permanently. And rather than the new circumstance thwarting our travel plans, we viewed it instead as an opportunity to visit two countries which had not been included in our original itinerary – Japan and the USSR.

There was one further consequence of our changed plans – without having to go north of the 20th parallel we received all our tax back. Our six months' sojourn in Australia had fallen equally into the end of one tax year and the beginning of another, and in both years our income happened to be just within the non-taxable bracket. When we eventually arrived back in Belfast a tax refund would be awaiting us. It was a welcome bonus.

Ironically, although our stay in Australia had been of a far longer duration than for any other country on our trip, it was the country we explored the least. That is the major drawback when necessity forces you to put down roots in order to earn a living – you might get closer to the local people, but the ability to move around at will is greatly curtailed. We did contemplate spending a month touring around but we could not make that month fit in with the other parts of our return itinerary, and so, somewhat regretfully, we crossed the Nullarbor Plain on the Trans-Australian Railway and within two days of arriving in Sydney found ourselves on a flight to Auckland. We could always come back and see Australia again, we told ourselves. But even then we knew instinctively that things are never that simple.

New Zealand
(31 October – 30 November 1977)

We only stayed in Auckland overnight. Because we would be returning there for our onward flight, we decided to leave any exploration to our second visit. Furthermore, we were intending to hitchhike, and given the unpredictable nature of this mode of travel we knew it was prudent to plan for our return with at least a day or two to spare.

We relished being able to resort once more to hitchhiking. There is always a great sense of anticipation when, having arrived in a new country, you reach your first pitch and eagerly raise your thumb to the approaching traffic. New Zealand, at least on that first day, was not to disappoint us. Six lifts, with little delay between them, took us to Waitomo Caves by early afternoon. After finding a reasonably-priced chalet we booked in for the last tour of the day to the Caves. Unfortunately, we were the only ones wanting to go and our Maori guide spent the first few minutes grumbling about it being a waste of his time with only two. However, he then thankfully desisted, gave us an informative tour, and by the time we surfaced he was more than friendly, his former irritation completely evaporated.

The following day we received a quite unusual lift. As a large furniture lorry passed us in a swirl of dust we only thumbed it half-heartedly, assuming it would not stop. However, it suddenly pulled in just ahead of us and the driver beckoned us over. We climbed aboard without even asking where he was bound, as we were happy enough to accept even short lifts. After we had motored about a mile down the road the driver turned and scrutinised us carefully.

"I never give lifts, you know."

Sheila and I exchanged alarmed glances.

"Why did you decide to stop for us, then?"

He stared out through the windscreen for some moments, concentrating on the road ahead, before finally responding.

"I have a large removal job on and my assistant couldn't make it. I assume that in exchange for the lift you'll both help me out?"

I was somewhat surprised by the presumptiveness of the man, but what could we say? Anyway, I mused, perhaps it will not take that long and he might prove good company. And who knows, despite the man's obvious aversion to hitchhikers, maybe we can leave him feeling more amenable to our fellow-travellers. When I nodded our consent he seemed to relax somewhat and then began to tell us about himself. There was no dialogue – he was not really interested in us – it was more of a monologue, but we did not mind, for at least we were moving.

While he told us about his varied interests, it was evident that his one overriding concern in life was his removal business. He had built it up entirely through hard graft and seemed intensely proud of his achievement. He made it perfectly clear that nothing else could ever be as important to him.

"Even my wife understands that."

I was somewhat surprised to hear that he was married, for I had imagined that a man with such a single-minded pursuit might not find much room left in his life for a spouse.

"What does she think about your occupation?"

"She knew what to expect when we married. I told her that I considered my job, and even this lorry, more important than our marriage."

He said it matter-of-factly; there was no hint that anything was amiss in their relationship. He was simply explaining reality as he perceived it, and we could only assume that his wife was content enough to fit in with his needs. He fell silent for a few minutes, then indicated with his thumb to the raised sleeping area behind our heads, more specifically to a small shelf in the furthest recess.

"There are pictures of her in there, if you want to see them."

"It's okay . . . maybe later when you stop."

But he was persistent, as if these photographs held some great importance to him.

"No, get them out. You should find them interesting. It's pictures of her . . . in different positions."

What! Both Sheila and I looked at each other, stunned. What type of character were we travelling with! Over the past few miles I had begun to feel more at ease, despite my initial doubts, but now those doubts returned with a vengeance. Yet his face showed no sign of menace, no concealed smirk, no hint of the 'dirty old man' ready to flap open his raincoat.

"Go ahead – they're just behind you."

With some trepidation I did as he instructed and retrieved a slim wallet. I flipped open the cover to reveal perhaps two dozen colour photographs. Sheila and I exchanged disturbed glances again. I carefully removed the photographs from the wallet, wondering what delights of the Kamasutra would now be arrayed before our gaze.

It was all I could not to burst out laughing! A laughter that would have been largely of relief, I must admit, for the 'her' in these photographs was his precious lorry! And, sure enough, each photograph showed 'her' in "different positions", some quite unusual. He leaned over and when he spoke it was with a voice filled with pride.

"See that photo there – yes, that one. That was a really difficult job. The house was way out in the hills with no proper road leading down to it. And you can see how far she's lying over to one side – there just wasn't a flat bit of ground anywhere. The more we loaded the furniture on, the more she leaned over. I thought she was nearly gone at one stage."

He was so engrossed in describing his photographs that I found myself glancing anxiously at the road ahead, but luckily we seemed to have the highway to ourselves.

"And see that next one . . . the house was tucked away under an embankment and we had to haul every bit of furniture up by ropes. You can see one of the ropes tied to the bumper. Then that one there . . . yes, that one . . . just look at the narrow gap I managed to negotiate the lorry into – just between the house and the barn. The owner of the house said it couldn't be done."

That would not have been the wisest thing for any householder to say to our companion, I mused. I did wonder, however, just at what stage in each job he halted his labours and rushed to get his camera out. What did the householders think about it? As we perused the photographs – more specifically, as he talked us through them – I had to admire him for his dedication to his work. This man had certainly found true job satisfaction.

We finally arrived at the house – a modern dwelling standing by itself amid attractive countryside. Although there was no-one about, the door was unlocked. The driver led us on a tour of the rooms, during which he ascertained from the owner's written instructions where each bit of furniture was to go. Having completed his overview, he lowered the tailgate of his vehicle and beckoned me over.

"You can help me unload all the heavy stuff. But first we'll get these tea chests out and perhaps your missus could unpack all the ornaments and small items which are inside?"

And so for the next three hours he and I unloaded the entire contents of the lorry and gradually filled up the empty rooms, while Sheila carefully unpacked all the ornaments, toiletries and bundles of clothing. At first she found it a little disconcerting – for in a sense she was intruding into the personal world of some unknown family – but eventually she just got on with the job and thought little more about it.

By the time we were ready to depart there was still no sign of the owners. As we drove away I reflected on what had been a quite unusual situation. For us, that is, though obviously not for our driver; it was clearly just another routine job for him – we could tell that because he never even asked to take our photograph.

Although we felt that we had more than repaid our lift we were to be disappointed by the way the encounter was to end. We arrived in the outskirts of Wanganui in the early hours of the morning, feeling distinctly tired and looking forward to a good sleep. Our driver pulled his vehicle into a wide lay-by, announced that this was where he was going to spend the night, thanked us for our assistance, informed us that he was sure there was a youth hostel in the centre of the town . . . then bid us goodbye! We stared at him in astonishment, but only a bland look returned our gaze. Surely it would not have been that much of an imposition to drive us into the town centre – especially as there was not a single other vehicle on the road! I felt like saying something sarcastic but desisted.

We slung our backpacks onto our shoulders once again and proceeded along the deserted street in the direction of the town centre. It seemed to be miles away and my irritation at our driver's lack of consideration increased with each hundred yards we trudged. The fact that Sheila was pregnant added to my worries – I soon had myself convinced that this could not be good for her.

Just then a taxi exited a side-street directly in front of us, the driver looking as surprised to see us as we were to see him. As we had no idea where the youth hostel was located we had little option but to get the taxi to take us there. So our six man-hours of hard work had been rewarded by having to fork out our precious money for a taxi fare!

When we found the hostel it was in total darkness; indeed, rather than looking shut for the evening it appeared to be closed down permanently. The taxi-driver, to his credit, did not wish to leave us standing there on the pavement and banged on the door repeatedly until a bleary-eyed girl eventually opened up. She did not even bother to enter into conversation but turned and walked away again. We entered the building, and using only the light filtering in from outside, managed to find ourselves a place to bed down.

· · ·

Having crossed from the North Island to the South Island we hitched down along the coast – and thereby joined the ranks of the 'loopies', the name New Zealanders gave to tourists who 'did' the South Island by travelling down one coast then looping round to return along the other. But one 'must see' item on any loopie's itinerary was certainly on ours – Milford Sound.

None of the numerous tourist posters depicting Milford Sound had made any mention of the sandflies which infested the shoreline. The view, especially of Mitre Peak, was as beautiful as the photographs proclaimed – indeed, even more so – but it was as much as I could do to take our own photographs before following Sheila at a brisk run away from the water's edge, constantly wafting the biting insects away from my face.

We had another problem at Milford Sound – a light rain was beginning to fall and we had nowhere to stay. Well, that was not strictly true: we could have taken a room in a local hotel, but that would have set us back over $30. A passer-by told us that workmen were busy on what he took to be some kind of hostel not that far away, so we trudged along the road as the drizzle gradually became rain and, by the look of the darkening sky, threatened to develop into a downpour. The hostel, when we reached it and spoke to the workmen, had been built primarily for Milford Track walkers. Unfortunately it was not due to open for another fortnight. Seeing our disappointment and our frequent and apprehensive glances skywards, one of the workmen, who hailed from Edinburgh and was nicknamed 'John the painter' by his colleagues, motioned us to one side.

"Act as if you're both away off down the road again. We're due to lock up soon and I'm usually last to leave. When you see a van go past wait a few minutes then come back here – I'll hang around until you return."

We did as he instructed and some twenty minutes later 'John the painter' allowed us to become the first hikers to avail themselves of the hostel and its facilities. Although the rooms had no beds, they were newly decorated and the electricity was connected up. John searched around and brought us a heater, despite our insistence that it was unnecessary.

Milford Sound is located in Fiordland National Park, which, in conjunction with the neighbouring Mount Aspiring National Park, forms a spectacular wilderness area within the Southern Alps of the South Island. Although most of the area is wild and untamed, a few popular walking trails intrude into some of the more accessible, yet still scenically rewarding, corners of the Park. The most popular of all is the Routeburn Track, a 24-mile traverse which climbs to Harris Saddle, a spectacular gateway between the two parks. More importantly for us, given our minimal hiking equipment, the Routeburn was perhaps the easiest walk in the region. The trail was well-made, well-marked and at strategic points along the way there were accommodation huts. At the time of our visit these would be open but not manned.

An early morning bus from Milford Sound took us to the Divide – so called because it is the lowest East-West pass in the Southern Alps – from where we commenced our walk to the first hut on the Routeburn, pleasantly situated beside Lake Howden. The following day's walk took us to Lake Mackenzie Hut, its setting even more idyllic. Sitting on boulders by the edge of the sparkling, crystal-clear water we felt very much at peace. Unfortunately, clouds soon descended and the surrounding mountain panorama was eventually obscured, the cloud cover also bringing a sudden chill to the air.

The hut was only a third full of trekkers and a camaraderie quickly developed, which was fortunate as the following day it rained without let-up and all the hut's occupants resigned themselves to staying a second night.

Throughout that second day a steady trickle of trekkers joined us in the hut and by evening the small lodge was full to bursting. Yet, it was a gregarious crowd and the damp evening was spent in boisterous banter and the inevitable swapping of travel notes. We found ourselves endowed with something of a celebrity status because of our Asian trip, for many of the other hikers were intending, or dearly wanted, to travel in Asia and we were inundated with requests for information – not that we minded being given this welcome opportunity to reminisce.

The following morning the rain had ceased, although the surrounding vegetation still sparkled brilliantly from the after-effects of the previous day's deluge, while the sun struggled valiantly to make an appearance. The steady patter of raindrops from both the nearby bushes and from the eaves of the hut provided an unusual contrast to the silence we had experienced upon our arrival. When we finally set out on the trail again we were frequently sprayed with miniature rain showers as our backpacks brushed past overhanging foliage.

The vegetation thinned out, however, as we made our way up to the pass known as Harris Saddle, and we lingered there to gaze upon the beautiful views of the Darran mountain range. The highest portion of the Saddle was covered in snow and this added to the scenic splendour of its wild location. Our senses finally sated we continued onwards, past the Routeburn Falls Hut and then on to the one at Routeburn Flats. We were almost at the end of our food supplies, so even if the rain came down in another deluge we would have to complete the Routeburn the next day.

We need not have worried, for the following day was dry and sunny and it was an easy stroll to the main road where we boarded a bus to Queenstown. We had been told that a park warden would collect our hut fees at the end of the trail but no-one had appeared by the time the bus arrived. We did feel somewhat guilty about this, although we were secretly pleased to have saved some money. Our guilt and our pecuniary satisfaction were both premature, however, for a few miles later a warden boarded the bus and relieved us of NZ$12.

· · ·

"It's out there! Quick – I can see it!"

Startled, everyone in the room hastened to the main door and within seconds the multinational occupants of the youth hostel were clustered outside in the cold air in small groups, gazing rapturously at the sunset-lit mountain peak which towered majestically above them. At last – after a frustrating two-day wait – we could view Mount Cook, New Zealand's highest mountain, free from its obscuring cloud. The sight, as with so many of the world's great mountains, was truly awe-inspiring: the ragged outline revealed to optimum advantage by the beautifully clear sky; the ridges down its flanks seemingly chiselled out to perfection; the surface of the snow in parts taking on an almost waxen appearance in the fading sunlight; here and there cornices appearing to hang in impossible suspension; and the perfect triangle of a rouge-tinted summit perched atop like a royal crown.

As the last embers of sunlight finally abandoned the mountain face to the encroaching darkness, everyone slowly trooped back into the hostel. There was a palpable sense of contentment among all the mountain-climbers and backpackers staying at the Hermitage, and those with a proclivity for checklist tourism ticked off another of their 'must see' sights.

The following morning we were provided a second opportunity for wonderment, only this time, instead of the rose-tinted gloss of the late evening sunset, the mountain now shone with a pure whiteness which dazzled our eyes with its pristine brilliance.

· · ·

Hitchhiking in New Zealand, despite the promising start, did not prove to be consistent. On a number of occasions we were left standing disconsolately by the roadside for hours. Indeed, after getting a lift six miles out of one town we had to bus it back again five hours later when it became obvious that we were completely out of luck and it was a choice between returning to town or possibly sleeping rough. Twice we had no option in the matter, on one occasion bedding down in a field, the other in the draughty porch of a Presbyterian church. As these delays were all the more frustrating because time was so precious, we resorted to buses and even the occasional train to maintain our momentum.

But when we did obtain lifts they invariably proved to be more than compensating. A Canadian family in a hired combi-van squeezed us in and an hour later we accompanied them on a steep walk to a viewpoint overlooking Fox Glacier. Another lift, which took us to the thermal area of Rotorua, was in a converted 1951 bus which crawled along and had to have its radiator refilled every twenty miles. One of our last lifts, as we came close to Auckland again, was from an extremely laid-back member of a commune located on the Coromandel Peninsula. But perhaps our most amusing lift was from a pleasant old man who seemed to have spent his entire life within his own locality and who we imagined must have rarely stopped for hitchhikers. He took us a mile and a half further along the road, and when he heard that we were heading for the next town, looked at us in consternation.

"That's a good thirty miles away, you know. That's some distance – I hope you make it!"

Fiji

(30 November – 10 December 1977)

Even though we landed at Nadi around 9pm the day was still extremely hot. The high temperature, coupled with the surge of hotel and taxi touts which met us outside the airport, was reminiscent of Asia, but we managed to elude this hopeful throng by taking public transport into town where we quickly located budget accommodation.

However, given the short time we would be spending on Fiji, our sojourn in Nadi could only be brief. We wanted to locate ourselves in a village, preferably by the sea, and when we learned that there were cheap cabins available in the Sovi Bay area we departed from Nadi the following day. Unfortunately, when we had alighted at our destination – Vatukarasa village – and enquired after accommodation, villagers told us that no such cabins existed. We had either got off the bus at the wrong place or we had been misinformed. Nevertheless, some of the people who had gathered around us said that they would be quite happy to put us up in their homes and when I initially turned down this idea because I considered it an imposition, they insisted, explaining that it had been done for other visitors.

And so it was that we came to stay in a *bure*, the traditional thatched family dwelling of the native Fijians. This large abode is a one-roomed affair, although some members of the family – and ourselves – were provided with a little extra privacy by the use of hanging screens. On our first day we repeatedly endeavoured to get our hosts to accept money but they consistently refused it, and finally indicated that an acceptable alternative would be to buy groceries for them from the village's only shop.

We began to understand this seeming disdain for money as we slowly settled into village life, for the inhabitants were basically self-sufficient, with produce such as breadfruit, yams and sea foods readily available. Unfortunately, our image of a people living at one with nature was dented somewhat when they revealed that what they wanted us to purchase from the shop were items such as sweets, cigarettes and sugar; indeed, plenty of sugar, for they shovelled it into their beverages by the spoonful.

The Fijians' easy-going lifestyle and their self-sufficient, non-commercial approach to daily sustenance had one major drawback, according to an articulate member of our host family. The indigenous Fijians were outnumbered by Indian settlers whose ancestors had been brought to the island in the 19th century by the British to work the sugar plantations. Many of these Indians were, unlike the indigenous people, firmly established in trade and commerce, which in turn had brought them much power and influence. The indigenous Fijians had watched this development with increasing unease, and our informant told us that suspicion and antagonism between the two communities was growing. He had real concerns for the future, he told us sadly.

"I would like us all to share this island in peace, but there is trouble coming, I can feel it."

The village, like its setting, was incomparably idyllic: thatched huts set snugly amidst lush vegetation; a perfect cone-shaped hill standing sentinel in the background; the constant yet unobtrusive sound of waves lapping on the nearby shoreline; the shrill laughter as children chased each other everywhere, mongrel pups yelping at their feet. Up on the main road, where it crossed a river, a bridge was put to constant use as a diving platform by squealing children and frolicking teenagers.

For us it brought back fond memories of beaches in India, Thailand and Malaysia, and once again we found ourselves spending hours walking along the shoreline, ostensibly searching out shells but in reality simply revelling in the pleasure of being in such a place. Often we were accompanied by village children, infectiously full of an irrepressible *joie de vivre*.

The local men were proud of their fishing expertise and frequently netted more than the small fish which provided much of their diet – one afternoon they brought back four turtles, an octopus and a stingray. The women invited us to observe the cooking, but the thought of the unfortunate creatures being killed in front of our eyes was too much and we declined.

While the children were slim and agile many adults were extremely chubby, a circumstance no doubt contributed to by the starchy nature of some of their staple food, and of course the vast amount of sugar they consumed. And there was plenty of food on offer – the father of our host-family had died shortly before our arrival and our stay coincided with one of the feasts which was to be held every fifth day over a lengthy period following his death.

But all too soon we had to announce our intention of departing. Our host-family insisted upon gathering together – all twenty of them – for a group photograph, with Sheila given the privilege of nursing the youngest member. The night before our departure the men of the household presented us with the traditional *yagona* (*kava*) farewell drink, passed to us somewhat solemnly in a shallow dish. It left a strange, bitter taste in our mouths, but we tried not to reveal our reaction least we gave offence, though it probably would not have occasioned them much surprise.

It was sad to leave the village, especially to be parting from our host-family, for their hospitality had been generous to a fault. As our bus took us out of sight we wondered just what changes might eventually be forced upon Vatukarasa village if those tourist cabins ever did get built.

We visited Suva, the capital, before we left the island, and it provided ample evidence that the development of tourist facilities was high on the agenda of local entrepreneurs. Furthermore, it seemed that some people in Fiji were preparing themselves for more than just tourists – the police station displayed wanted posters depicting the last uncaptured members of West Germany's Baader-Meinhoff terrorist gang. The world was definitely getting smaller.

New Caledonia
(10–19 December 1977)

Shortly after arriving in Nouméa, the capital of New Caledonia, we could tell it would be an expensive place, an impression confirmed when browsing the prices in shop windows. We were informed by one of the youth hostel staff that wages were not taxed, heavy duties being placed on goods instead. Nouméa had a large number of Europeans in evidence, and of course everything was so French, from the street cafés to the topless beach.

But when we set out to hitchhike the length of the island we began to uncover another side to life in New Caledonia. Surprisingly, in our encounters with local people my grasp of French proved to be more substantial than had ever been apparent on any of my visits to France. In France I had often encountered an aloofness because I was an English-speaker, or at times I would be bombarded with words spewed out like machine-gun bullets, leaving me totally bewildered and speechless – indeed, I sometimes imagined that that was the intent. But here, the indigenous people in particular intuitively knew just what was required: slow, careful speech, with difficult words kept to the minimum. They also genuinely *wanted* to know about us – and our mothers, fathers, brothers and sisters – so they persevered, and in response I persevered. And always our efforts at communication were punctuated by their warm laughter and nonverbal encouragements, hence my confidence grew and to my great surprise I found that I had retained more French from my school-days than I had ever imagined.

Many people befriended us as we hitchhiked around the island. One French woman and her daughter went out of their way to take us to locations we would never have got to without transport. At one village some local children took us to a good spot near the beach where we could sleep, then proceeded to light a fire to keep the mosquitos away. When later that evening it began to rain the children returned, dragging an adult by the hand. He was the caretaker of the local school and they insisted he open it up for us, which he did without hesitation. Indeed, he arrived back at the school some twenty minutes later with blankets and pillows.

One of our encounters went less smoothly yet ended happily. Stuck for over three hours trying to get a lift on a road along which only a trickle of cars had passed, in desperation we hailed a passing bus. At the bus's final destination, after all the other passengers had departed, the driver tried to charge us 700 French francs each, and yet we knew that the price from Nouméa to our present location – well over twice the distance we had just travelled – was only 760F. Suspecting an attempted rip-off we queried the amount and the driver and I engaged in a lengthy argument. He claimed that the majority of buses on the island were privately owned and the government enforced fixed prices on long distance journeys only, not short ones. We began to feel he might be telling the truth; for his part, he acknowledged that his price must seem high to backpackers. Finally, he announced he would take 700F for the both of us and then insisted upon buying us a drink. The encounter at least put a bit more polish on my French, and before leaving us the driver offered some useful advice: the post-bus, which only ran once a day, was also subsidised by the government and was much cheaper than privately-owned buses.

We found much of the scenery of New Caledonia, even along the coast, disappointing. As well as that, nickel mining played a large part in the island's economy and many parts of the island bore the scars of Man's assault upon the landscape. It was only as we travelled to the northwest of the island, particularly around Hienghène Bay, that the scenery began to impress us. Indeed, not far offshore in the bay lay some vegetation-covered rocky islands with such bizarre shapes early missionaries had given them descriptive, and suitably appropriate, names, such as Le Sphinx and Les Tours de Notre Dame.

Back at the youth hostel in Nouméa our last night on New Caledonia was to be disturbed when one of the hostel's voluntary helpers crept into the girls' dormitory and tried to molest one of the sleeping hostellers. The entire hostel was roused by the screaming, but another member of staff shrugged off the incident, explaining that the culprit was "always doing that", as if it was quite acceptable. The next day we flew to a country where such behaviour at a hostel would be quite unthinkable.

Japan
(20 December 1977 – 4 February 1978)

Walking through the streets of Tokyo, with its unbelievable press of humanity, brought back memories of being in a major Indian city. But there the resemblance ended, for while the image imprinted by Delhi, Calcutta or Bombay was of a bustling poverty, Tokyo presented a pushy, all-embracing affluence. Almost without exception the inhabitants were neatly, often immaculately, attired and the backdrop of glittering shopfronts and huge attention-demanding neon advertisements served only to reinforce an overpowering spectacle of wealth.

And yet behind this affluence and ultramodern commercialism there were occasional glimpses of an older, more formalised culture which seemed quite at variance with the brash materialism. Nowhere was this better epitomised that during some of the social encounters we witnessed taking place in the street. Japanese etiquette requires that when two people met they should both bow, the one of lower social ranking making the deeper movement. A complex set of expectations surrounds bowing, including the depth and duration of the bow, and the appropriate response. For example, if one person maintains their bow for more than the normal few seconds, it is deemed polite to bow again, upon which the other person might also bow again. This often results in a long exchange of progressively shallower bows, with the result that both individuals would be bowing up and down like two budgerigars. Somehow this would have seemed less incongruous if it was occurring in a village setting where everyone was dressed in kimonos and robes but when it occurred against a backdrop of skyscrapers, honking taxis, smartly-dressed commuters and busy restaurants, it looked strangely out of place.

However, despite such distractions, for most of those first days in Tokyo we had our minds focused on one primary objective – the purchase of warm clothing. It was a shock to experience the sudden change from the heat of

179

New Caledonia to the chill of a Japanese winter. Our next priority was to visit the Japan-Soviet Tourist Bureau to book our boat tickets to the USSR, as well as have the Soviet and Polish embassies arrange the necessary travel visas through Eastern Europe.

• • •

From Tokyo we took a train north to Nikko, whose famous shrines – some of them the most beautiful in Japan – have made it one of the country's most popular tourist destinations. As our first glimpse of Japanese religious architecture we were suitably impressed. While staying at the hostel there we also hitched to nearby Lake Chuzenji and back, partly to experience what it was like travelling around unencumbered by backpacks. Yet although we also hitched without much difficulty to our next destination – the area around Mount Bandai – we were already beginning to reassess our original itinerary, in which we had wanted to include the northern island of Hokkaido. For a start it was cold, too cold to stand long at the roadside waiting for lifts. The sun invariably disappeared each day by 4pm, but even during the period it remained visible the coldness could penetrate every layer of our clothing with ease. To compound matters, many of the cars travelling north were bunged full of occupants and luggage, the drivers waving apologetically as they passed. We could have taken the train, but the fares charged for the distances we hoped to cover would have stretched our budget to the limit.

Yet the winter conditions did provide compensations. Minutes after our lift to Mount Bandai dropped us off close to the youth hostel, we met a member of the hostel staff returning there by snow-mobile and we gripped tightly onto the back seat of his machine as it weaved its way around trees and launched itself into space over mounds. We watched the approach of these mounds with some alarm, convinced that their covering of snow was of insufficient depth to prevent our skis from snagging themselves upon hidden obstacles. But nothing went amiss and, quite exhilarated by our excursion, we arrived safely at the hostel, the driver grinning broadly, though in a friendly manner, at our obvious anxiety. The youth hostel itself was warm, both in its temperature and in its welcome.

Close to the hostel was spread out a fantastic array of coloured lakes, known collectively as Goshikinuma, the colours ranging from deep emerald to jade and turquoise. The colours were due to copper minerals, while the lakes had been created in 1888 when a volcanic eruption had blown the top off Mount Bandai and the resultant debris altered the course of two rivers, forming dozens of lakes, ponds and swamps in the process. The scenic wonderland thus created, however, had cost the lives of 500 villagers. Our visit to Goshikinuma had fallen on Christmas Day and we went for a dreamlike walk through the snow-white woods which surrounded the lakes, our collars wrapped tight as protection against the occasional drenching we received when snow which had accumulated on overhanging branches eventually slithered to the ground.

When the time came to leave this beautiful place another snow-mobile ride took us back to the bus-stop. A fierce blizzard was blowing and although we attempted to thumb any cars which passed we boarded the bus without hesitation as soon as it arrived. For a twenty-minute ride to the nearest town it was disconcertingly expensive, and by the time the journey had ended the blizzard had worsened, forcing us to take a train to our next destination, Sendai. In the hostel there we tried to accept the reality of our situation. The intense cold, the shortage of empty cars, the prohibitive cost of train and bus fares . . . continuing northwards was just not realistic. Reluctantly we decided to turn south and seek warmer weather. This is not as strange as it might seem, for the territory of Japan stretches 3000km south from latitude 45°N to almost touch the Tropic of Cancer, and the weather can vary widely throughout the four main islands which make up the bulk of its landmass. As one guide book pointed out: "There can be blizzard conditions in Hokkaido; sunny, crispy-cool weather in Tokyo and Kyoto; mild Mediterranean conditions in Kyushu; and pleasant warmth in Okinawa."

But before we would commence our revised itinerary there was one sight we wanted to see – the famed islands of Matsushima Bay, which lay not far to the north of us. We hitched successfully to Shiogama, arriving there just as an excursion boat was leaving. With the sun's warmth endeavouring to counteract the cool breeze out in the bay we spent an enjoyable hour being motored around the more photogenic of the islands, some eroded into natural arched bridges and most of them covered with twisted pine trees.

• • •

With my latest attempt at conversation with our driver only achieving yet another of his apologetic smiles, I turned and gazed through the car window. Outside in the rapidly failing light the streets seemed busier now, with an ever-increasing flow of homeward-bound workers adding to the bustling shoppers. What an urban sprawl, I reflected. We had been hitching most of the day without having seen any real green-belt areas to break up this endless chain of shops, garages and factories, all advertising their presence with the ubiquitous multicoloured signs. We did not get a sense of leaving one town or of entering another as the map would have us believe; instead, the journey south through the main island of Honshu resembled travelling down one extremely long and busy street. It was as if this major trunk road possessed some secret magnetic quality, acting much as a river does in attracting along its length population settlements and indistinguishable commercial zones.

I noticed the driver nodding and smiling at us again and ceased my musings to concentrate on another sentence. Without exception all the drivers who stopped for us exhibited a desire to converse, but language proved a frustrating barrier. The hauntingly feminine voice of a Japanese male Kabuki singer provided our background music as the car made its way through the traffic. I returned the driver's smile and pointed to the audio cassette player.

"That singing is very good. It that Japanese classical music?"

But only a look of friendly incomprehension greeted my statement. By the movements of his hand he indicated for me to try again. I realised the task was probably futile but made a renewed effort.

"Very nice music. Very different from Japanese pop music."

A dawning understanding broke upon his features and his face beamed.

"You like?"

"Yes, it's very good."

His hand reached out and before I could prevent him he flicked out the cassette tape and presented it to me. I waved my hands in protest.

"No, no! I just said that I *liked* it; I didn't mean that I *wanted* it. I just said that the music was very good. Put it back and play some more."

182

But he pushed the cassette insistently into my hands and his smile became even broader.

"Okay, understand. Yes, understand. You take. Present . . . for baby."

We all smiled then and I respectfully accepted the cassette, the driver and I exchanging the customary head bows in the process. He settled back once more to concentrate on his driving, a contented look upon his face. Well, I mused, at least he had understood our earlier conversation.

We found the generosity of the Japanese almost embarrassing at times. Most drivers who stopped for us – and they were always male – wished to present us with a gift of some kind, and we always hoped it would be something relatively small and inexpensive. One driver had given us a varied assortment of bandages and plasters and would have emptied out the entire contents of his dashboard pocket if we had not managed to prevent him. Another, while we were intending to cross Tokyo Bay from the Boso Peninsula, had driven us to the car ferry and then, before we realised what he was doing, dashed over to the ticket office to purchase our tickets. Some stopped halfway through their journey to buy us tea and cakes. Yet another, a Japanese Christian, told us that he had initially driven past us, but then stopped and prayed, with the result that "God told me to come back for you".

The most unusual, but admittedly most useful, present was from a driver who had repeatedly glanced over at me in bewilderment as I studied a thick road atlas of Japan, which I had retrieved from the door pocket. I was trying to find a good place for him to deposit us, one which would provide us with the best opportunity for onward travel.

"You told me you do not speak Japanese?"

I looked at him in surprise.

"I'm afraid I don't."

"But that book is in Japanese!"

"No, no. I can read maps. Any map."

"But that map is in Japanese!"

How do I explain this, I wondered. I spoke slowly and carefully.

"No, I do not speak Japanese – but I love maps. I could sit all day looking at a map."

"Do you know where is Nagoya."

"Yes, it is there. And there is Kyoto; there is Nara; there is Kobe; there is Okayama . . ."

I suddenly felt I might have overplayed my expertise, for he stared at me in complete disbelief.

"You *can* read Japanese!"

"No, I can't. To me a map is a map in *any* language. Once I know where places are, the *words* on the map don't matter. It's the *roads* that matter."

He muttered to himself and returned to his driving. I glanced anxiously at Sheila, worried in case I had in some way offended him, but she just shrugged her shoulders.

When we came to the end of our lift, however, he was all smiles. But before we parted company he reached back into the car – most drivers got out of the car with us – retrieved the atlas and presented it to me. I immediately demurred, almost in a slight panic, for while the atlas would have been a real asset I had no desire to deprive the driver of such an expensive item. He continued to insist and I continued to resist. Finally he pressed the book into my hands in a manner which brooked no further argument.

"If you can read Japanese maps so well, you must keep."

And with a final courteous bow he returned to his car and moments later had rejoined the busy traffic.

• • •

The slowing down of our present vehicle woke me from my reverie. The driver edged his way into a parking spot and all three of us exited the vehicle. He helped us manhandle our backpacks out of the boot, energetic handshakes were exchanged and then we were alone on the pavement. Well, alone that is save for the throng of homeward-bound Japanese who gave us curious but friendly glances as they passed. I flicked through the Japanese Youth Hostel Handbook, a few flakes of snow dampening the pages.

I had deliberately withheld our actual destination from our driver, because of another aspect of Japanese helpfulness. On our first week of hitchhiking, when the last driver of the day would ask where we were bound and we mentioned a youth hostel, he would invariably reply: "I go there too." At first we thought these were simply lucky coincidences, but it was just *too* coincidental and we eventually realised that the drivers were not necessarily going to the hostel at all, they were deliberately *taking* us there.

It put us in a dilemma. In the chill of the winter evenings it was admittedly pleasant not to have to undertake a long trudge from the centre of town to a hostel, but our hitchhikers' ethics told us it was unfair to take advantage of such generosity, especially when we realised that we could be taking drivers well out of their way. And so when asked where we were going we now said that anywhere near the town centre would be fine. A few minutes later I would innocently enquire where the driver himself was from and where he was bound. If his reply indicated that he could deliver us nearer the hostel – if we knew its rough location – then I might suggest an alternative drop-off point. If he indicated a completely different direction then we would continue to insist that close to the town centre was perfect and not risk impinging any further upon his generosity.

The hostel turned out to be another ryokan, a traditional Japanese inn. The Japanese Youth Hostel Handbook – our most useful purchase in Tokyo second only to our warm clothes – bulged with hundreds of addresses, although only a few were actual purpose-built official youth hostels. The majority were affiliated accommodations such as municipal hostels, temples, private houses and ryokans. At this particular ryokan, however, we were to encounter once again one annoying aspect of this affiliation arrangement. As on other occasions we bought bread, eggs and other perishables as we made our way to the 'hostel', basing our purchases on the clear indication in the handbook that this particular ryokan had 'self-catering facilities'.

When we were booking in, the woman in charge asked us if we also wished to pay for supper or breakfast. When we replied that we would make our own, she looked taken aback. "Not possible," was her adamant reply. We pointed to the handbook entry, and then to the framed certificate hanging over her desk, which proclaimed for all to see in both Japanese and international symbols that her ryokan had self-catering facilities. She studied both – as had the staff in other similar hostels – shook her head as if seeing it for the first time – as had the other staff – then looked up sternly before pronouncing her final decision: "Not possible."

The confusion over this matter was frustrating, for although we quite enjoyed these prepared meals, it was obviously much cheaper to make our own, and it often left us having to hitch the following day with items such as milk or eggs – easily spilt or broken – in our backpacks. In all the hostels we stayed at we never saw Japanese youth making their own meals, and at those few hostels where it was actually possible they would watch with great curiosity as we did so, as if it was something quite alien to them.

Nevertheless, it was evident that Japanese youth made good use of the hostel network, and for a very practical purpose: the hostels provided them with an excellent means of escaping the confines of family life with its numerous restrictions. In the hostels we found it curious that all the girls sat separately from the boys. There was occasional interaction between the sexes but it was always conducted in a very polite and proper manner. One positive outcome of all this proper behaviour was that Japan was a remarkably safe country as regards personal safety. We thought it very creditable that teenage girls – girls who admitted to us that they came from very protective homes – were able to go hostelling the length of their country without any fear that they would be hassled by males.

We ourselves experienced some of that sense of security. Arriving at one train station in the early hours of the morning we had decided to lie down – feet to feet – in our sleeping-bags on a station bench rather than attempt to search out accommodation. We had just fallen into a doze when a very inebriated male – one of the few drunks we ever encountered – squeezed himself between us and seemed set to doze off too. We were uncertain what to do and I watched anxiously as his head swayed about for some minutes before he finally crashed down bodily onto Sheila's legs. I was in the process of getting up when two policemen suddenly appeared, manhandled the unfortunate man off the bench, and then trailed him unceremoniously out of the station. Having presumably deposited him outside in the cold and damp street they returned, smiled politely to us and indicated that it was now safe to go back to sleep.

It was also safe with respect to property; one foreigner told us with conviction that if you left your backpack down in a public place and did not return for it until the next day it would still be sitting there, if it had not already been handed over to the police.

186

. . .

The centre of Kamakura had been closed to cars and our driver apologised for not being able to take us any further. As we made our way through the dense crowds of people we saw the sense in prohibiting traffic. Being the New Year celebrations everyone was dressed in their best clothes, many women brightly attired in colourful kimonos. After checking in at the hostel and relieving our aching shoulders from the weight of our backpacks, we joined the crowds and wandered around the temples and shrines. At one shrine, as we made our slow progress sandwiched amidst the chattering worshippers, a loud voice instantly caught our attention.

"Hey, you two! Over here!"

Startled by the unexpectedness of the shout, we turned and saw a Westerner sitting on a tree stump. As we squeezed our way across to him he took a few swigs from a half-empty bottle, his face glowing. I wondered what the Japanese thought of him sitting on the stump, as other tree stumps in the vicinity had small offerings deposited on them. Seemingly oblivious of the pressing throng of people he jumped up and greeted us like old friends.

"Hey, am I glad to see you two guys! Like some *sake*? No? Come on, I insist on you both coming back to my place for a meal. No 'buts'!"

The three of us retraced our steps to the entrance, receiving curious looks for the way our new acquaintance strode briskly along, gesticulating freely and taking the occasional gulp from his bottle.

"Never worry about them! They all know me around here; they're well used to me by now. Anyway, they're happier if I act a bit odd; they can accept me better."

Feeling somewhat perplexed by this statement, we followed him through the suburbs and then up a narrow lane which ascended to a row of wooden houses perched on a hillside overlooking the town.

Our new companion, Danny, was an American and he and one of his compatriots, Jim, had lived in Japan for some years, both men having also married local girls. Danny could speak several Japanese dialects and earned his living as a translator. His young son was a beautiful child who had more of his mother's features than his father's. Once we had consumed a filling Japanese meal, Danny suddenly stared pointedly at us.

"Tell me – what do you honestly think of the Japanese?"

We described all those encounters through which the Japanese had revealed their hospitality and friendliness. Danny nodded repeatedly as we spoke.

"I agree, they're basically a very friendly people. But did you not sense an element of *duty* about it all? A feeling that it just wouldn't have been proper for them to leave a foreigner standing by the roadside? They're a very dutiful people, you know."

We admitted that this was possible, but we had not quite perceived it that way. Danny was obviously impatient to enlarge, however.

"I've been in Europe and there the more you attempt to speak a country's language the more it pleases the locals. But here it's the very opposite – the more helpless you act, the more they'll help you. The more you flounder about asking for things in the shops, the warmer their smiles become. Because then you're a known quantity to them – you're a foreigner, a *gaijin*, and to the Japanese there are only two types of people in the world: themselves and *gaijin*. Labelling you as a *gaijin* serves to reassure them. But if you try and enter deeper into their society then the more they fear your intrusion. When I speak fluent Japanese to them in the shops I rarely get a smile, and when Jim and I were trying to marry into their midst, Christ, what a battle we had, what an upset we caused . . ."

He paused as if reflecting upon some private memories.

"And the Japanese are so enigmatic. I'm sure you've contrasted the public untidiness with the private fastidiousness?"

Indeed we had. We had been amazed at the sheer complexity of rules regulating cleanliness and tidiness. The hostel at Goshikinuma, for example, had three types of slippers for residents' use. One pair for wearing on any of the stone or wooden areas downstairs, especially near the entrance hallway. Another pair which you changed into for use on matted surfaces or when going into the bedrooms, and a final pair which you stepped into when going into the toilets. Rows of abandoned slippers clearly indicated the demarcation lines between the different sectors. At another hostel there were even instructions pinned up in every dormitory giving precise details on how to fold blankets correctly before storing them away in a cupboard – with the rounded folds always to be facing outwards, never the rough edges.

And yet in the alleyways running behind many food establishments, which otherwise looked spick and span from the front, rubbish of all types spilled over the ground in an unsightly and unhygienic mess. To us there seemed to a glaring inconsistency between the ritualised etiquette surrounding cleanliness and this other reality.

While we listened to Danny I found it difficult to determine just how much of what he was saying was accurate, and how much was borne out of that growing isolation which so frequently erodes the expatriate's fondness for his adopted country of domicile and increases his wistfulness for the ways of his country of birth. I recalled the elderly man who, despite our protestations, had walked with us up a long and steep hill so that he could show us the whereabouts of a hostel. Or the family who, when they saw us arrive at the former hostel next door to them only to find it shut down, had brought us into their own home, sitting us down to a meal without delay. Or the vanload of workers who drove us into a motorway café area and insisted on asking around the other drivers until they found us an onward lift. Or the warden at the temple hostel in Koyasan who followed us into a nearby restaurant and paid for our meal. Surely all this generosity and friendliness was the result of more than mere duty?

Before we rose to leave, Jim had already departed for his own house, somewhat sick with drink, and we watched him sway slightly as he descended the path. It all had a touch of sadness about it.

• • •

As I scrambled with undignified haste up onto the low wall and endeavoured to stretch myself as high as I could – in order to position my camera over the fencing which ran the length of the stonework – I was aware that passers-by were staring at me with incredulity. And well might they exhibit surprise, for this was unusual behaviour even for a *gaijin*, especially in the centre of a major city – in this case Hiroshima. Yet there was a purpose to my seemingly odd behaviour. We had been walking towards Hiroshima's most famous, or infamous, landmark – the Industrial Promotion Hall, which had been directly under the atom bomb of 1945. The only major building not obliterated by that devastating and horrifying explosion, it was allowed to remain as a permanent symbol of the cataclysmic destruction. Commonly referred to as the 'A-bomb dome' it was a gaunt and broken shell of a building, quite symbolic of the agony of the city's inhabitants.

Although the sky above us was perfectly clear as we neared the building, I noticed that a large black cloud was fast approaching which would soon conceal the sun. I also realised that the lighting effect which would result could provide a dramatic backdrop to the scarred building. We quickened our pace as I hurriedly got the camera ready, yet despite our speed it was patently obvious that we would not make open ground in time, where I could get an unhindered view of the dome. Hence my ungainly behaviour which had startled the passers-by. However, my embarrassment was worth it, for the effect was as dramatic as I had imagined: any former colour in the brickwork now vanished as the entire structure became a pure black brooding silhouette. The gaping holes of the windows added to the ghostly appearance while the dome itself, with its exposed ironwork, took on an eerie, even sinister, look. An intruding street lamp seemed like the antenna of some menacing creature from outer space. Yet, ironically, the creature which had seen fit to wipe out over 70,000 human beings in a matter of seconds had been man himself.

My photographic activities were later to cause a stir among a number of young males in Saiko youth hostel. I had been woken by the usual 'dawn chorus' chattering which emanates from all Japanese youth in hostel dormitories – a situation we had grown accustomed to but one which often caused intense irritation to other travellers. However, I had barely opened my eyes when my attention was caught by a red glow which suffused the entire room. Being in a top bunk, I raised myself onto one elbow and glanced through the nearby window, which overlooked beautiful Lake Saiko. The sky was a brilliant blaze of fire and the tranquil waters of the lake seemed to be of blood, not water. I leapt out of bed, pulled my camera from my backpack and flung open the window. Unfortunately, just under the window sat the roof of the kitchen area and no matter how far out I stretched I could not capture the fiery scene without part of the hostel intruding. I knew what I had to do – climb out onto the kitchen roof, even though it was covered in snow and my feet were bare. Then, I suddenly remembered that it was not just my feet which were bare. I also became conscious of the silence which now pervaded the room and I spun around. Every face in the dormitory was staring at me, with a look of either astonishment or horror, or perhaps both.

Japanese hostels were generally warm, if somewhat airless at times, and the plentiful supply of blankets made for a snug night's sleep. Despite this, however, young Japanese males were in the habit of getting into bed with almost all their clothes on, whether from custom or modesty I was never sure. I, on the other hand, normally slept without clothes and furthermore felt that when waking up on a cold winter's morning it was better – psychologically, as much as anything else – to know that you had warm clothes *to put on*. So there I was, standing by the open window – entirely in the nude.

I was caught between my embarrassment and my desire for a photograph. As an instant compromise I dashed back to my bunk, donned a pair of underpants, proceeded to climb out through the window, and then endeavoured to capture on camera the sight which even in those few precious seconds of delay had already lost much of its intensity. When I finally re-entered the room to hurriedly brush the snow from my frozen feet the silence was still in force and it was to be some time before the former chattering resumed. One guide book gives the words to use when trying to get Japanese youth to be quiet: "shizukani sh'te kudasai", if you want to be polite, or "shizukani!" if you want to be more forceful. I had discovered an alternative method which produced instant results.

• • •

As we stood near the toll gates we knew that one lift should suffice to take us back to Tokyo. From Tokyo in a few days' time we would take the short train journey to Yokohama for the boat to Eastern Siberia, and from there it was the Trans-Siberian Railway all the way back to Europe. The next lift, then, would be the last on our trip. Indeed, with a child on the way, it was probably the final occasion we could indulge ourselves in this mode of travel. I actually felt quite sad, as if some essential part of my life was finally drawing to a close.

As cars passed we thumbed hopefully, though we were in a predicament. Because of the way the toll gates were spread out, only those vehicles heading for the gate nearest us would be in any position to pull in, which meant that we were missing the majority of potential lifts. We could not proceed any further towards the motorway and if we retraced our steps it would take us onto the dangerously fast approach road to the toll area. It was a bad pitch, no doubt about it. And yet it was the only pitch. Our last ever lift and we were stuck!

But one vehicle *was* prepared to stop, a vehicle we had certainly not thumbed – a police car. It drew up alongside and the two occupants slowly got out. Our last attempt at hitchhiking was certainly trying to stamp itself as memorable, I mused ruefully. One officer scrutinized us for some moments with a serious expression etched upon his features.

"This is bad place for hitchhike."

I quickly scanned our surroundings just to check one last time that we had not strayed into a pedestrians-prohibited area, and shrugged my shoulders.

"I know."

He continued to stare at us, then at our backpacks; his face, however, did not reveal any hint of animosity. That was a good sign at least, I mused. From his introductory remark I surmised that he probably spoke reasonable English, an impression soon confirmed.

"Where are you going?"

"Into Tokyo. We are at the end of our holiday in Japan. A very enjoyable holiday."

The flicker of a smile crossed his face. He contemplated us for a few moments more.

"We are going into Tokyo also. Do you want to come with us?"

We could tell this was no trick – he was offering us a genuine lift. So our hitchhiking days were to end in a police-car! How appropriate. I gave the officer a courteous bow and reached for the straps of my backpack.

"We do. Thank you very much."

As we slowly merged in with the Tokyo-bound traffic I settled myself comfortably into the seat, and, perhaps because I was conscious of the significance of this particular lift, I passed most of it reflecting on my hitchhiking experiences.

Hitchhikers would normally identify two primary motivations behind their mode of travel: firstly, the fact that it was the cheapest way of getting around a country, especially for those travelling on a shoestring budget; and secondly, the conviction that it was also the best way, for it brought you into a more direct contact with local people than most other methods of travelling. Few travellers got the opportunity to live in people's homes in the countries they visited, but sitting in a family car observing all the interactions taking place – whether between man and wife, parents and children, or the children and the world at large – was surely the next best thing. If the car's occupants were talkative and open and you reciprocated with interest, then there could be few subjects left untouched: politics, cultural mores, the state of the economy, marriage, sex . . . everything from the local to the global. You could learn what people really thought about their country's leaders, and often what they thought about your own. And, just occasionally, a good rapport struck up within the confines of the family car could end with an opportunity to live, even temporarily, in the family home.

Contrary to many people's image of it as being a purely free-for-all affair, hitchhiking possessed its own unofficial set of rules and expectations. The primary one, and one surprisingly adhered to by most hitchers – though admittedly with varying degrees of willingness – was the maxim: first there, first served. If you arrived at a pitch to find someone already in position you automatically walked beyond their pitch, leaving them with the first opportunity of stopping a car. There was nothing to make hitchhikers abide by this convention, but those who did not comply were treated like pariahs, and as the chance of running into other travellers again while 'on the road' was surprisingly high – whether at the next pitch or in hostels – no-one liked to be ostracised.

The expectation to take up a pitch beyond other hitchhikers already in position was sometimes amended, though usually by collective agreement. Once, while standing at a motorway slip-road in Germany, so many hitchhikers began to accumulate that no driver could have stopped for fear of being swamped by a deluge of hopefuls. Quite spontaneously a few of us began to discuss our common predicament. Then the others were brought in on the discussion, and, in our own unique international forum, practical decisions were taken. Half of the group, those who had arrived last, would vacate the roadside and rest up in the nearby woods. This would allow the others to spread out, thus increasing their chances of a lift. As each hitchhiker proved successful, everyone would move down a place and the last vacant pitch would be taken up by one of those sent to rest. The 'agreement' would be explained to any newcomers in the hope that they would also comply.

There were also general rules to follow when trying to maximise the chances of a lift, some learned through experience, some gleaned from other hitchhikers. Stand where you could be clearly seen. Stand where it was safe for cars to stop and preferably at a place where cars have had to slow down – a long open road which allowed vehicles to belt along was quite useless. Be prepared to walk long distances to reach the best pitch. Do not look threatening to drivers by hiding your face deep within an anorak hood. Do not react to rude gestures given by vehicle occupants, for a more sympathetic driver might be following behind. As dusk approached stand in a well-lit area, and never near dark bushes. Lay your rucksack down flat with its smallest end facing the approaching traffic, as drivers were often concerned that bulky packs, especially those with frames, could damage their upholstery. Carry a sketch-pad and thick black marker with which to indicate your destination when stuck at confusing junctions. Before getting into any car make sure you knew roughly where the driver was going; some lifts could actually slow you down by leaving you stranded on backroads, or by depositing you at bad junctions. If uncertain, study the map during the journey and ask to be dropped off at a more suitable pitch before your driver reached his destination. As for pinning small national flags onto your pack, there was much debate on this topic: some hitchhikers liked to think of themselves as free from such narrow categorisations, others felt that being seen as foreign visitors could appeal to some drivers' sense of obligation.

The loneliness which was often experienced, however, could be the most unsettling part, especially for those hitchhiking for the first time. While some females did hitchhike alone, it was wiser and safer for them to hitch in pairs. Indeed, they often had more chance of getting a lift that way, for many drivers felt that stopping for a single female carried too many risks. And a few male drivers who readily stopped for single females often did so with ulterior motives. But for male hitchhikers, two was a crowd. Only the most generous of drivers, or those well used to giving lifts, cared to stop for two males and two large backpacks. For a male, then, hitchhiking was generally a solitary experience, especially if they were hoping to cover long distances.

And when standing for hours alone at the roadside you were free to dwell upon anything which came to mind: concerns over whether you would get to that day's intended destination; musings about what those left at home might be doing at that very moment; the preoccupation with totting up how much of your precious budget had been spent and what remained; and often the question which sooner or later was bound to arise – what the hell am I doing standing for hours at the side of this bloody road, why on earth did I ever decide to subject myself to this blinding rain/burning sun/biting wind/chilling breeze when I could be sitting snugly in the pub back home with friends?

Yet, the attraction of hitchhiking was that such doubts could be dissipated in an instant with the securing of a good lift, or the arrival at your pitch of an attractive member of the opposite sex. Hitchhikers could approach other hitchhikers without it being seen as an intrusion, and often 'on the road' encounters provided travelling companions for the days, even weeks, ahead.

Sometimes you were lucky to have an experience which could be repeatedly brought to mind on those occasions when you needed to counteract all the doubts. Mine had occurred on my first venture onto the European mainland. I had been standing just outside a pleasant French village, in the shade of an old farmyard wall which was almost hidden behind a thick covering of ivy. Not far away on the other side of the road a few teenage girls sat chatting on a patch of newly mown grass, one of them every so often emitting a shrill laugh and lunging playfully at her comrades. But as for me, I was far from laughing, for I had been standing at my pitch for over two hours, and the fact that the girls would look in my direction every few minutes made me increasingly self-conscious, as if I was the epitome of failure and worthy of their ridicule. With each passing vehicle I had grown more and more irritated. I perused my map yet again, trying to determine if another road might offer more possibilities, and mentally calculating how soon I would need to strike lucky if I was to reach my intended destination that night. But the map offered no real alternative to staying put and hoping my luck would change.

When it increasingly seemed that it would not, I was confronted with that inevitable question: was I wise in the head doing this?

Then, at the height of my doubting, instant clarity and peace of mind had suddenly enveloped me, like the experience of *satori* in Zen enlightenment. Why was I getting so obsessed with reaching some *other* place, I asked myself, when I had never even been in *this* place before? Why was I allowing my thoughts to be dominated by frustration at an unfulfilled itinerary, when I should be letting my senses savour to the full all that my present surroundings had to offer? I had left home seeking different places, different people – well, *every* place I would travel through could offer just that, if I would only let it; even where I now stood was a different place. In that moment my mood changed and I became fully accepting of whatever would come next. If I was to be stranded there for the night, so be it; I could easily bed down in the woods behind me. Who knows, I might even pluck up the courage to approach the teenage girls and try out my rudimentary French. Whatever might happen I would accept it as all being part of my experience. As luck would have it, a car stopped five minutes later and I did make my intended destination that night. But I had learned a valuable lesson – *every* place one arrived at offered the possibility of being a worthy destination.

The unpredictable nature of hitchhiking was reflected in the variety of places you could find yourself spending the night, though this was also part of its attraction. While youth hostels were good places to rest up, wash clothes, meet other travellers and gather travel information, at times the vagaries of travelling 'on the road' did not facilitate an arrival at a hostel. Sometimes it was easier to bed down in a wood or on a beach. Some of my overnight stops remain vividly imprinted on my memory. Such as when police ejected me from Frankfurt railway station where I had been hoping to sleep and a young German girl invited me to accompany her to a nearby squat, only to be woken by blinding torchlight a few hours later during a police search for drug-pushers. Or while sleeping rough with others on the beach at Finale Ligure on the Italian Riviera only to find riot police watching us from the promenade and being told by them that if we were still there the following evening we would get 'acquainted' with their truncheons. Or the time I slept in a field in Switzerland during a spectacular but frightening electric storm, during which so much rain fell that my plastic bivi-bag, with me inside it, slid ten yards down a field towards a river, carried along by a sudden torrent of water.

Hitchhiking did have its potential dangers, unfortunately. Thankfully, assaults and murders were extremely rare, but the possibility of being picked up by the wrong driver was always there and caution had to be exercised at all times. Yet, it was not always possible to predict what could happen when you got into any vehicle. My worst experience occurred in 1974 while hitchhiking to Yugoslavia with Sheila – her first and only encounter with this mode of travel prior to our departure for Asia.

A driver had dropped us at a bad junction east of Frankfurt; 'bad' in the sense that the only safe – not to mention legal – place to rejoin the autobahn was at a slip-road a few miles from where vehicles then had the option of going in one of two quite different directions. This always created difficulties. Drivers obviously had no idea in which direction you wished to go and you always feared that even those who might have been willing to stop would take the easy option and drive on past. Ordinarily, if you knew there was a major junction ahead, even if it was a few miles away, you would walk to it, but that was not possible on motorways.

I got the sketch-pad out of my backpack and was marking out our destination when a screech of brakes caused me to look up sharply. A car had skidded to a halt just beyond us and an arm was beckoning urgently from an open window. We gathered up our backpacks and hurried towards the vehicle. As we got closer we could see that its occupants were three US servicemen, one sitting beside the driver, the third in the rear.

"You guys want a lift?"

I was conscious of the major intersection up ahead and had no wish to be caught out going the wrong way.

"Are you headin' in the Nürnberg direction?"

"Sure – anywhere you want to go."

Now, such a reply should ring warning bells to any hitchhiker and I instantly hesitated. But before I could query the driver's unusual response he leapt out and squeezed our packs into the boot of the car. I quickly glanced at all three servicemen in turn, hoping my intuition would guide me through this dilemma. As the driver returned to his seat I tried to convince myself that they were probably friendly enough. And yet I felt a nagging irritation, as if this decision was in reality being forced upon me. And when hitchhiking, especially if there is the slightest question about personal safety, nothing should be allowed to prevent you from exercising caution. Notwithstanding such principles, however, moments later we found ourselves in the back of the car as it rejoined the main traffic. I looked around the three men again.

"You going into Nürnberg yourselves?"

The driver shook his head and spoke with some distaste.

"Nah. Don't like the godamned place."

Apprehension engulfed me. What had we got ourselves into? Damn it, why didn't I hold back when we had the opportunity?

"We're just out for a drive. We've got two hours before we're due back at base, so we'll burn you for an hour, drop you off, then head back."

'Burn you for an hour'? What on earth did that mean? As if sensing my uncertainty the driver laughed mischievously.

"Burn rubber, man. Watch!"

With a sudden lurch the car surged forward, moving out into the overtaking lane with such momentum that Sheila and I were thrown bodily against one another. As the vehicle accelerated I glanced anxiously at the other occupants. In no time at all we were hurtling along at 90 miles per hour, until we eventually caught up with the line of cars ahead and had to slow somewhat. Even though these other vehicles were still going far too fast for my liking, it was a relief to have them act as a break to our headlong momentum. But it was only a temporary reprise, for the driver, suddenly seeing a gap in the inner lane, swerved across it to position himself on the hard shoulder. What the hell was he up to!

Once more the vehicle gathered speed. For a moment I could not believe what was happening – the idiot was using the hard shoulder as his overtaking lane! Everything then assumed the appearance of a surrealistic nightmare, a collage of juddering images: the roar of the car . . . the occasional gleeful yell from one of the three servicemen . . . the startled looks on other drivers' faces as we sped past . . . Sheila's hand grimly clutching my arm . . . interspersed with my frantic glances ahead to ascertain whether the hard-shoulder was actually continuing, for I knew that it occasionally narrowed and even at times ceased altogether depending on the terrain.

But eventually we had overtaken the mass of traffic and had the road to ourselves . . . for the moment at least. The car rejoined the inner lane and for some reason slowed down to about 70 miles per hour. At first I thought that without any traffic in sight the driver did not have the same need to impress, but I was soon proven wrong. He nudged the front passenger and indicated to the dashboard pocket.

"I could do with a snort."

The passenger straightway opened the dashboard flap and retrieved a small notebook, the empty shell of a ballpoint pen, and a tightly-folded envelope. He carefully opened the envelope and tapped the open edge on the centre of the notebook, a white powder falling out as he did so. Then, using the ballpoint shell as a conduit he inhaled some of the powder sharply into his nostril, immediately throwing his head back and breathing deeply.

"Jesus, that's good stuff!"

His head returned upright and swayed a little as he savoured his stimulant. The driver nudged him again.

"Well, don't hog it, man! Hold the wheel."

And before our startled eyes the passenger took hold of the steering wheel with one hand while the driver used his new freedom of movement to repeat his friend's exercise. He too threw his head back against the car seat, but, more terrifyingly, the front passenger again did likewise. And we were still hurtling along at 70 miles per hour! With an involuntary movement of my hand I forcefully pushed the driver's head upright again, which caused all three servicemen to break into near-hysterical laughter.

"Are you guys scared?"

I did not know what I felt more: fear or anger. Anger at them and anger at myself. But the fear was there too, and for some reason it was accompanied by a terrible feeling of guilt: it was all my fault that Sheila was now going to meet her death needlessly in a mangled car on a German autobahn. I held her closer and could feel her fear. Perhaps sensing this, or perhaps because he had placed others in this situation before, the driver seemed to read my thoughts.

"Are you scared of dyin'?"

I tried my hardest not to reveal my terror.

"I was hoping to give it a few more years of contemplation."

He laughed cynically, as if he saw through my pitiful attempt at nonchalance.

"Man, we three did a stint in 'Nam. When you've been to 'Nam, you realise that death isn't such a big deal."

Maybe not for you selfish bastards, I cursed inwardly. He glanced over at me, but I decided not to pander to his self-centred philosophising and pointedly stared out through the window. As if in response he slowly began to accelerate.

The next few miles were a nightmare, a nightmare which I really began to believe could only have one outcome. I even had a vision of the police trying to identify our bodies from the strewn contents of our backpacks. Then, the unexpected happened. As we hurtled past the other vehicles one of the servicemen turned his head sharply.

"Hey, man, I think we just passed one of ours!"

The driver suddenly braked and the car went into a skid which he luckily managed to correct. We all looked over and, sure enough, another car with an American serviceman at the wheel was cruising along sedately. Our driver drew alongside the other vehicle and the front passenger wound down his window, gesticulating as he did so to the other driver. For a moment the latter did not respond but then his window too began to lower. Our passenger shouted across the narrowing gap.

"Would you give these two guys a lift!"

Their uniformed compatriot, a black sergeant, looked at us sombrely but did not respond.

"Well, yes or no? We have to head back to base!"

At last the faintest sign of a nod was returned and the vehicle slowly began to move towards the hard shoulder, our own car following a few yards behind. When both vehicles were stationary our driver jumped out and, a little unsteadily, unloaded our backpacks from the boot.

"Best of luck, you guys – see yah around!"

As we slowly carried our backpacks over to the other vehicle our former lift, with demonic yells emanating from all three occupants, suddenly shot straight across the road and headed for the low hedge which separated our section of motorway from the one going in the opposite direction. With a loud scrape the vehicle bumped over the obstacle and within seconds was accelerating rapidly out of sight. We stood dumbfounded for some moments, not just because of the manner of the servicemen's departure, but undoubtedly still in shock from our experience. Finally I turned to our new driver.

"Look, I apologise for this. You don't have to give us a lift. It was wrong of them to force this upon you."

He stared at me expressionlessly.

"You want a lift or not? If you do, get in."

And now the inevitable urban sprawl which announced that we were approaching a major city also indicated that our last lift was nearing its end. After our exchange of courtesy bows with the two motorway policemen we re-entered the neon-lit bustle of downtown Tokyo. When we called at the Russian embassy to collect our visas, for which we had to provide a total of eight passport-sized photographs, the staff expressed disquiet that few of these seemed to have been taken at the same time – but when we explained that they were all we had left and that for us to obtain new ones would necessitate going without an evening meal, they relented and accepted our assortment.

USSR
(4–18 February 1978)

We had *never* experienced seas like these before. As the ship ploughed its way across the Sea of Japan to Nakhodka in eastern Siberia the ocean stubbornly resisted our progress every inch of the way. Our cabin was unfortunately right up in the bow area and as the seas lifted the prow into the air it seemed to hang suspended for ages before pummelling down onto the waves with a deep, shuddering boom which reverberated throughout the vessel. To lie in our bunks was only possible by hanging on grimly to the sides. Not that remaining in our bunks was our sole preoccupation, for every so often we had to stagger to the toilet to further empty our churning stomachs. We were thankful we had a cabin to ourselves, not just because it would be embarrassing to have others witness our agonised retching but because the sight of others engaged at the same endeavour would most certainly have triggered us off again.

A group of New Zealanders were also taking the Trans-Siberian Railway to Europe. During the period when our ship had travelled parallel to the coast of Japan, where the roll was at least acceptable, initial contact had been established with some of our fellow-travellers, but once the Sea of Japan was encountered eventually all passengers retreated to the seclusion of their cabins. Our determination to eat everything set down before us – especially as the meals had been included in the price – was soon defeated by the equal determination of the heavy seas to ensure that anything we consumed was speedily ejected again.

At one stage we ventured up on deck in the forlorn hope that a fresh breeze would help alleviate our constant nausea, but the sight which met our eyes instilled fear instead. The waves which leapt around the ship were enormous, and those which crashed against the vessel did so with a vengeance. White spume frothed and spewed from the raging sea as if from some rabid monster. If the vessel had seemed fragile when judged from below decks, to our consternation it now seemed decidedly puny, tossed around in the seething maelstrom as effortlessly as a cork. When a sailor spotted us out on deck he immediately ordered us below, gesticulating angrily at us and then at the waves with a meaning which required no translation.

I had often assumed that the expression 'to turn a sickly colour' was a fanciful description not meant to be taken too literally, but we soon realised just how accurate it could be. But above all, as we were tossed up and down on our bunks without respite, I agonised over the effect I felt sure this violent assault upon our bodies must also be having on our unborn child.

Yet eventually the turbulence of the seas abated and the vessel settled down to a more tolerable motion. And, as if by way of making amends, the last few tranquil miles to landfall were completed during sunset, the vessel having to break its way gently through a ghostly field of glistening ice.

•   •   •

The Trans-Siberian is the longest train journey in the world. The track stretches nearly six thousand miles from Moscow to Vladivostok on the Pacific coast. As Vladivostok itself was closed to the prying eyes of foreigners our boat landed at Nakhodka, which lay further east along the coast.

The train we boarded at Nakhodka was surprisingly plush and, thankfully, reasonably warm, for the chill night air had managed to penetrate every inch of our clothing as we made the short transfer journey from the ship. And although we were more than glad to be on solid ground again, the motion of the train, as it made its way north to Khabarovsk, created its own problems and we found it difficult to get any sleep. With a full seven days of train travel ahead of us before we reached Moscow we hoped that our adjustment to the new motion would come quickly. Not that we would be constantly on the train for a full week, for we planned to break the journey at Irkutsk and Novosibirsk.

All travellers journeying within the USSR had to be accompanied by a representative of the Soviet tourist bureau, *Intourist*, and the guide allocated to both ourselves and the New Zealand group was a friendly girl in her twenties who spoke flawless English. As part of the service the *Intourist* rep would arrange for transfer to hotels, and any stopover included a local bus tour. Some of the New Zealanders felt this was merely a way of preventing tourists from wandering around on their own, but given that the temperature out of doors was –20°C, we were quite content to be shepherded around in a warm coach. The tour of Khabarovsk lasted an interesting three hours, although its highlight was when we actually vacated our vehicle and went for a walk along the frozen Amur River, endeavouring to communicate with local people who were fishing at bore-holes made in the river's crust, their exposed locations protected to some degree by windbreaks made from roughly-hewn blocks of ice.

The next three days were spent on board the train, sitting beside our window and watching the white wilderness of the Siberian forest – the *taiga* – pass by. We had worried that the snow scenes might begin to pall after the first day, but we were to find ourselves constantly enchanted by the beautiful landscape. No two scenes were ever the same, and every bend of the track revealed yet another stunning combination of forest and snow drift, occasionally supplemented by a wooden house half-buried under its white blanket.

The dust and dirt thrown up by the passage of the train meant that even by the end of our first day a deposit of grime had accumulated on the windows which threatened to make any photography well-nigh impossible. When I discovered this I was dismayed by the thought of not being able to capture on camera the magnificent scenery we were passing through – over five thousand miles of it. On our second day, therefore, I resolved to do something about it, for a solution seemed quite obvious.

Each carriage possessed a large cylindrical water boiler – the railway's version of a samovar – used for making tea. As the train slowed down for the first stop of the day I filled a large beaker with hot water, then quickly alighted when the train finally came to a halt. Our guide had indicated that she did not like us attempting to leave the train at the smaller stations, although it was unlikely that any of the foreign passengers wished to do so, for some of the halts lasted for only a few minutes and it would have been easy to get left behind.

Nevertheless, with the beaker in one hand, an old face-cloth in the other, and taking care not to tumble headlong on the extremely slippery and icebound ground, I made my way along the outside of the carriage until I reached the window of our compartment. Then, to the astonishment not only of those Russians gathered around but my startled fellow-passengers peering out from adjoining compartments, I jumped up and down in the snow – there being no raised platform at this particular stop – reaching as far as I could in an attempt to clean the glass.

My task accomplished I returned to the train to face the angry admonitions of our *Intourist* guide, who, when she realised that I was going to insist on doing this at the first stop of each day, finally accepted that her best course of action would be to assist me, by being on hand each morning to explain to any railway officials what I was up to. The other travellers viewed the matter with some amusement, but one of them later said he regretted not doing the same, for seemingly we were the only ones who managed to obtain worthwhile photographs of the beautiful Siberian *taiga*.

• • •

As we made our way past other compartments on our way to the dining car we would nod greetings to the Russian passengers, but to our disappointment they usually remained quite sombre, even somewhat dour. One particular circumstance, however, was to change all that. The New Zealand group included a couple travelling with their two young boys, aged six and eight, and by chance we accompanied them on one excursion to the dining car. Any reserve the Russians had displayed towards the foreign adults vanished completely in the presence of the children. The two boys were hugged, shaken hands with, presented with numerous metal badges, bombarded with sweets . . . at every compartment. It took us an extra half-hour to reach the dining car, but it was well worth it, for once the ice had been broken, courtesy of the children, a good rapport was soon established with many of our Russian fellow passengers.

When it came to the dining-car staff, however, no such ice-breaking had been required. They were friendly to a fault and seemed to thoroughly enjoy interacting with the passengers. While the meals were served promptly and without fuss they still managed to find time to converse with the tourists, and the dining-car soon became – for the foreigners at least – a focal point where food was not the only attraction. One of the staff in particular, an ever-cheerful, somewhat overweight and matronly woman, was the epitome of a *babushka* figure – personifying all the warmth and earthiness of Mother Russia, someone you imagined could alleviate all your ills by just one of her heartfelt embraces. To everyone's delight the staff frequently broke into song, sometimes singing tunes of a sprightly nature which had you itching to dance, at other times crooning ballads which revealed the deep melancholic sadness so much associated with the 'Russian soul'. And our hosts sought no more recompense for all their attentions than the laughter and gaiety which so frequently reverberated around the dining-car. When the train arrived at Irkutsk, where all of the foreigners, ourselves included, were scheduled to disembark, there was a widespread and genuine regret to be parting company with such open-hearted and down-to-earth people.

• • •

Our arrival in Irkutsk was at 1.30am, and another *Intourist* guide met us and got us quickly onto a waiting bus; it had to be quick because the temperature was now –34°C. To his consternation, when we arrived at our hotel there seemed to have been some mix-up, for the doorman refused us entrance. While the two men argued, the rest of us waited on the outside porch, stamping our feet and blowing on our fingers in an attempt to ward off the bitter cold, and growing ever more anxious at the unexplained delay. Finally, to everyone's relief, we were allowed inside and once rooms had been allocated no one lingered to socialise but made hurriedly to prepare for bed.

The main attraction of a stopover at Irkutsk was not the town itself but nearby Lake Baikal, the deepest freshwater lake in the world and the largest in Eurasia. Baikal freezes over from January to April so we were able to walk among its fleet of fishing boats, which rather than having been lifted onto dry land had been left on the lake to be seized in the grip of the frozen water. As we walked among their ghostly shapes it was as if we had entered some fairytale realm where everything had become eerily entombed in a frosty white environment.

At one stage during the day the temperature had dropped to –41°C, and shortly after our walk on Lake Baikal the *Intourist* guide had ordered me to return to the bus, pointing urgently at my face. When I looked in the driver's mirror I saw, to my consternation, that a perfectly round white spot, some five millimetres in diameter, had appeared on the tip of my nose. It was, so our guide informed me, the first stage of frostbite, and my face had obviously been too numb to notice its presence. It was actually only frostnip, but at that time I was unaware of the distinction and so over the next few hours I kept anxiously examining my nose, relieved when the spot slowly began to recede.

• • •

When we resumed our train journey the low temperatures were even more noticeable. This time our carriage was right at the rear of the train and we had to walk through twelve other carriages to reach the dining-car. The doors connecting each carriage were encrusted with ice and, paradoxically, felt burning to the touch.

Our next stopover was Novosibirsk, where our coach tour included a drive through Akademgorodok – 'Academic City – a sprawling collection of apartments and academic institutes which catered for the scientists who predominated among Novosibirsk's population. In the evening we were taken to the theatre to see a performance of Verdi's *Aida*, where our admiration for the magnificent sets and beautiful singing was tempered by the endless chatting indulged in by large sections of the audience. It was quite disconcerting, and when the performance ended and the foreigners burst into applause they were soon the only ones doing so, for the rest of the audience were already making for the exits. We were embarrassed for the cast, for we felt their efforts deserved at least one encore. It caused some interesting discussion among the foreigners later that evening.

"So much for the so-called Russian 'love of culture'."

"Yes, that was really strange behaviour."

"Maybe not that strange."

"How can you say that? It was downright rude."

"Did you see any cafés or bars in the town?"

"What's that got to do with it?"

"Well, where else are the locals supposed to go to on a freezing night?"

"You mean, you think they were just using the opera as a place to socialise?"

"That's what it looked like to me. If they'd had a choice, maybe the ones who nattered away all night would have gone somewhere else."

Ironically, Novosibirsk would be memorable to us not for this live performance of *Aida*, but for a cold, monumental memorial to the dead which we had been taken to see earlier in the day.

It was one of the most moving pieces of sculpture I had ever beheld. On one edge of a huge stone block, the figure of a mother grieving for her children had been painstakingly carved. The sculptor's skill was revealed by the very simplicity of his creation. With his subject's hand held despairingly to her mouth, you could almost feel the woman's anguish, sense her bewilderment. The sunken eyes, however, were what made the message of the sculpture so poignant, and the light covering of snow which had settled upon the folds of the woman's shawl added to the powerful effect.

Next to the pillar stood a wall upon which was inscribed the names of all those from Novosibirsk who had died during the struggle against Hitler. A flame burned in a receptacle close by and four young men in army uniform marched away in goose-stepping formation at the conclusion of their small ceremony of remembrance. We were informed that all young men from the local academies took their turn at participating in this guard of honour.

Despite the militaristic nature of the ritual I knew that the legacy of the war experience was far from being merely a concern of the Soviet authorities, but reached deep into the hearts and minds of the Soviet people. The Soviet Union had suffered more than any other nation during the war, with twenty million of its citizens perishing. The Soviets did not even call it the Second World War, but the Great Patriotic War, because to them it was a life or death struggle for their very existence as a people. Furthermore, as far as they were concerned, they bore the bulk of the fighting and the hardship, and most historians accept that the outcome of the European war was ultimately decided in Russia. We in the West have perhaps heard of the battles of Stalingrad and Kursk, but we know little else about what was in reality the greatest and most ferocious armed conflict the world has ever seen. And the cost in lives was staggering, on both sides. Eight out of every ten German soldiers who died during the war died on the Eastern Front. The

German army had already suffered horrendous losses, and had been driven out of most of occupied Russia – indeed, their retreating armies were being pursued into Poland and Romania – *before* the Normandy landings even took place. Whatever our opinions about their totalitarian government, the heroism and endurance of the Soviet people had saved more than just their own nation.

When we joined the next day's train the gaunt face of the statue was still on my mind as we settled into our new compartment and resumed our contemplation of the Siberian landscape, now supplemented by the rays of the morning sun flickering and dancing through its ghostly forest cover.

• • •

Back on the train again we were able to overindulge ourselves on caviar and Russian chocolates, courtesy of a few of our fellow-passengers who had fallen sick and felt unable to eat. We thought it highly creditable that the dining-car staff, rather than keep unused allocations for themselves, divided them out among the rest of us. We endeavoured to get them to take some of these luxuries for their families but they steadfastly refused.

One New Zealander had come on the journey with a surfeit of Cold War suspicions, and kept imagining that some of the most innocent-looking of the Russian passengers were in reality secret police. When a young student from Moscow learnt of this obsession, he used it to enliven his own journey. On one occasion, as he made his way along the passageway, he paused briefly beside the New Zealander and whispered softly to him.

"Don't look now, but the man three seats down . . . the one reading the paper. I know him . . . he's KGB."

As the New Zealander's eyes immediately – despite the warning – scrutinized the unsuspecting 'KGB agent', the young Muscovite continued on his way, giving us a broad wink as he did so, and endeavouring all the while to keep the merriment trembling his mouth from revealing itself in loud laughter.

• • •

But finally the longest train journey in the world was over and we were alighting at the terminal in Moscow. Hurried farewells were exchanged with our New Zealand fellow-passengers when they were dropped off outside a modern downtown hotel; we were booked into an older establishment, the *Berlin*. For Communist Russia, the *Berlin* was amazingly bourgeois in its decor and style, especially its restaurant. Indeed, it was reminiscent of those old films depicting the Tzarist period, before that way of life vanished in the wake of the Revolution.

The weather during our stay in Moscow was murky, and although snow fell frequently it never settled but turned instantly into a dirty slush. We dutifully trudged our way round the History Museum, the International Museum, the Lenin Museum and the Museum of the Revolution, but the most fascinating place of all was the Moscow Metro, for some of its underground stations were full of architectural surprises.

Red Square is dominated by both the Kremlin and St Basil's Cathedral. The latter is perhaps the more eye-catching, for its almost surreal assortment of spires and cupolas – not to mention their bright and unexpected colours – is quite startling. When we wandered into its dimly-lit interior we came upon a group of young females standing in a semicircle around a woman who was speaking to them in perfect English. As we stood in the background it soon became obvious that this was a class of *Intourist* employees out to practise their skills. The woman beckoned for one of the girls to step forward.

"Right – imagine you have a group of tourists with you now. Give them a talk."

The girl seemed quite flustered when she began speaking, and for a moment we wondered whether we should leave and not add to her discomfiture. However, we realised that she was probably unaware of our presence – we were standing in semi-darkness anyway – and her anxious eyes were only for her tutor. As she got into her stride she began to relax and soon a wealth of information was tumbling forth. She spoke knowledgably of the Cathedral's history; made reference to the legend that the Tzar was so impressed he had the architect's eyes put out to prevent him repeating his efforts for a rival; described in detail the small but magnificent paintings decorating the walls; and made a brief but fascinating digression about the work of Andrei Rublev, Russia's great 15th Century icon painter. When she had finished she looked quite relieved at having remembered all the information she had so expertly revealed. But she was in for a shock.

The tutor returned to her place in front of the semicircle, and again addressed the assembled students.

"Fine, you obviously remembered everything that you read. What did the rest of you think?"

Murmurs of guarded approval emanated from the other class members, but their hesitancy indicated that they suspected something was amiss. The tutor surveyed her students again, and then fixed her gaze upon the unfortunate student.

"Do you really think tourists want to hear *all* of that?"

The harsh tones of her voice added to the impact of her words – the young girl looked crushed.

"Tourists only *want* to know so much; only *need* to know so much. While you're standing here extolling the virtues of our great artists, they're impatient to be getting into the next room. Most tourists have a shorter attention span than young children."

Her tone relented somewhat, and she actually looked at the young girl with understanding and sympathy. We felt as relieved as the young girl herself seemed to be.

"Be concise. Give a good overview. Expand if you sense that the subject interests your audience. But if your audience looks restless, then you have said too much. Now – into the next room, and someone else can have a go."

We did not follow the group, not wanting to witness any more of the girls give their anxious presentations. Instead, we endeavoured to remain unseen in the background until the small, cramped room was quite empty, content to survey the magnificent paintings in the dim light and echoing silence.

• • •

It was not always possible to remain unseen in the background in Moscow, as we were to discover when we queued along with hundreds of Soviet citizens for our turn to view Lenin's embalmed corpse. As we slowly moved across Red Square towards the Mausoleum, feeling the biting cold penetrate our clothes, we noticed two guards approach our section of the line with resolute faces and hurried gait. I looked around to see what might be the cause of their obvious agitation but could discern none. Sheila whispered urgently into my ear.

"I think it's us they're after!"

"But why?"

The guards stood before us and began gesticulating at me, speaking gruffly in Russian we could not comprehend. Finally, no doubt exasperated by my lack of response, one of them grabbed my right arm firmly and pulled my hand from the warm security of my pocket. What on earth was happening! Just then the man standing behind us in the queue intervened, speaking in perfect English.

"They want you to take your hands out of your pockets . . . and keep them out until you have left the Mausoleum."

So that was it? Why such a fuss? The guards, content that I had now complied with their demands, marched briskly back to their former positions. I turned to our informant and thanked him.

"But why? Would they consider it disrespectful if I stood in Lenin's presence with my hands in my pockets?"

"No, it is because of security; they are afraid you are concealing something with which you might damage the coffin."

And when we eventually got to walk past the recumbent form of the man himself, under the watchful eyes of yet more of his minders, I remarked to Sheila that his face looked as cold as my hands felt.

The following day we entered Poland by train. We had still a fair distance to cover before we returned home, but our minds were already focused there, wondering what we would find when we returned, and whether Northern Ireland was the best place to bring up our child. And we also wondered how our country's continuing misery would mould our own actions, for we knew there was no way we could turn away from it.

•　•　•

When we returned to Belfast it was to find that the cost of rented accommodation had increased dramatically during our absence and we felt that we would rather put our hard-earned money into a house of our own than into the pocket of some landlord. We finally located a suitable property, and, armed with our Australian tax rebates as a deposit, sat down with the estate agent who was to help us apply for a mortgage. I was handed a form to complete, on which I had to give details of my work record and earnings. I mentioned, somewhat naively in retrospect, that not only had we worked our way around half the world, but we had done so without incurring any debts and had even returned with savings in hand. Surely, I thought, that should prove our resourcefulness and ability to keep up with the mortgage repayments. The estate agent perused the completed form and then her eyes suddenly widened.

"Mr Hall, we . . . we can't send this! Especially the bit about your extensive travelling."

I was taken aback and for a moment was at a loss how to respond.

"But . . . surely it proves our ability to adapt. Would that not be reassuring to the mortgage lender?"

She looked at me in amazement.

"Mr Hall, the very fact that you and your wife went traipsing off around the world would only give most people the impression that you're both flighty."

I gaped in astonishment. Obviously not everyone appreciated the benefits of world travel.

Postscript

It was a remark by one of our two children which prompted me to write this book. One evening, in the middle of a quite unrelated conversation, our daughter Helen suddenly announced: "In a few years from now, I'm going to Asia too, you know." The 'too' was undoubtedly included as her way of reminding her mother and I that as *we* had been to Asia we could hardly try to stop *her* from going.

Her pronouncement did not come as a total surprise, for she was frequently in the habit of perusing our photograph collection and often plagued us with the same question: "Are you sure you can't remember anything else you haven't told me?"

When Helen announced her intention of going to Asia it caused me to search out the battered old diary I had kept throughout our journey. Originally intended merely as a record of all the photographs we took, its minutely-written lines had soon bulged with details of incidents, prices, destinations, hassles, pen-portraits of interesting characters, and not infrequently a report on the state of our stomachs. Even though our recollections of many of our experiences remain as vivid as if they occurred only yesterday, without that notebook I could never have written a detailed account of our journey, which is what I decided to do.

I wanted to reveal to Helen and her brother Christopher what the journey had meant for us, and what we felt about the people we met and the places we had passed through. I was unsure of its value, however, for I knew that people never stand still and places rarely remain unchanged. Would our memories mean much to those who travelled through the Asia of today?

As well as natural disasters such as earthquakes and floods, not to mention a terrible tsunami, man-made tragedies had also befallen most of the countries we had travelled through. There was the horror of 'ethnic cleansing' which engulfed the former Yugoslavia; the ongoing Kurdish unrest in eastern Turkey; the Iranian revolution, and Iran's devastating war with

Iraq; the Russian invasion of Afghanistan, the rise of the Taliban and the current engagement there of Western forces; turmoil in Pakistan, including an Islamist rebellion in the Swat valley; violence in India following the assassination of Mrs Gandhi; the Maoist rebellion in Nepal; Tamil insurgency in Sri Lanka; military suppression in Burma; terrorist bombings in Bali; army coups in Fiji; settler-native violence in New Caledonia; and the collapse of the Soviet Union.

Furthermore, having decided to begin writing, I was to find that there had been other changes too, far less dramatic, but which still caused me much regret. Browsing through travel guides in the bookstores, I sought to investigate how various locations had developed. Píthagorio was described as a "cluttered resort"; Celçuk had been "catapulted into the limelight of first-division tourism"; the "once small village" close to our family house on Samosir Island was now "a string of hotels and restaurants"; Nai Hahn beach was overlooked by a luxury hotel, the *Phuket Yacht Club*; Goa was now well and truly a package holiday destination; and to want to explore Delhi by air-conditioned coach no longer required a 'leap of imagination'.

I was almost put off my task. For if these places had changed so much I wondered if our children's generation would suspect my narrative of being misleading, or of engendering unnecessary regrets by pointing out what had once been but was now no longer. Yet however places might change – and change can often be economically beneficial to local people, irrespective of how much it might disturb a backpacker's idyllic memories – travelling will always be worth it for the people one encounters.

It is also evident that young people continue to be interested in the journey East. And to them, despite all the changes which have taken place, John Paiva's *Travellers' Ten Commandments* remain just as relevant, even if they might have become compressed somewhat into today's slick ecologically-minded maxim: take nothing but photographs, leave nothing but footprints. I would augment this, however, with two further pleas: take with you a open mind and leave behind you a sense of international friendship. For the real value of long-haul travel – one more valid now than ever before – is that it reveals to us just how much the peoples of our planet have in common and how fragile is the unique environment we all share.